M4 SHERMAN TANKS

THE ILLUSTRATED HISTORY OF AMERICA'S MOST ICONIC FIGHTING VEHICLES

MICHAEL E. HASKEW

Voyageur
Press

CONTENTS

INTRODUCTION

For three years, from June 1942 through June 1945, the United States Military Intelligence Service published the Tactical and Technical Trends series, booklets that discussed various aspects of the Axis enemies' strategies, tactics, weapons, and equipment during World War II. When useful to the publication's joint purpose of providing information and propaganda in the same package, it contained translated newspaper articles, memoranda, or other documents produced by the enemy. Such material, it was hoped, would provide insight into German, Japanese, or Italian perceptions of the Allied soldier and his weapons of war.

Published on October 7, 1943, Tactical and Technical Trends No. 35 included, among other items, a discussion of the Italian SM-82 bomber, the employment of German antiaircraft guns, the Japanese Model 99 machine gun, and the medical service of the German army. The issue also contained an article that was said to have been translated from a German newspaper story. It appeared under the heading "GERMAN COMMENT ON ENEMY TANKS."

The introduction, written by a staff member with the Office of Military Intelligence, reads, "A critical study of French, British, Russian and American tanks was published on 27 June 1943 in the German weekly newspaper Das Reich. It is interesting to note that the author does not attempt to minimize the merits of American tanks, particularly the General Sherman, and that he concedes that German soldiers 'know the dangers represented by these tanks when they appear in large numbers.'"

From the German newspaper to the American military intelligence bulletin, barely eight months had elapsed since the first US-built M4 Sherman medium tank advanced across a World War II battlefield. The event had taken place in October 1942, during the pivotal battle of El Alamein on the Egyptian frontier.

General Bernard Law Montgomery's British Eighth Army was sorely in need of tanks, many of its own already smoking wrecks and blackened hulls after months of fighting against the Axis Panzerarmee Afrika under the command of Gen. Erwin Rommel, who had become legendary during the fighting in North Africa and earned the nickname "Desert Fox."

The M4 Sherman was just becoming available in quantity at the time of El Alamein, and the initial thought was to train American tank soldiers to operate them and send a fully equipped 2nd Armored Division to Egypt under the command of Gen. George S. Patton, arguably the US Army's foremost authority on the deployment of the tank in battle. But time was of the essence. Training would take months, and the need was acute. The decision was made to ship the tanks directly to Montgomery's Eighth Army.

The Sherman initially compared favorably to the PzKpfw. III and IV tanks that made up the vast majority of German armored fighting vehicles in North Africa, and when the subject issue of Tactical and Technical Trends was published, Operation Husky, the Allied offensive in Sicily, was underway. Three years of hard fighting remained, up the Italian boot, into Normandy, across France and the Rhine to the heart of the Reich, and with the Soviet Red Army moving inexorably westward on the Eastern Front.

The Sherman was there on all fronts and deployed to the Pacific Theater as well. With the combat to come, this tank, produced in greater numbers than any other during World War II with the exception of the legendary Soviet T-34, became a legend in its own right. Its silhouette would become familiar to friend and foe alike—and both its proponents and detractors would evaluate its performance with great passion. For now, though, the Military Intelligence Division of the War Department in Washington, DC, chose to disseminate a German newspaper story that it

Opposite: A long line of M4 Sherman tanks equipped with Deep Wading amphibious equipment awaits the order to load into the belly of a Landing Ship, Tank (LST) at the French La Pecherie Naval Base in Tunisia for the journey to the beaches of Sicily. Operation Husky began on July 10, 1943, and involved approximately six hundred Allied tanks. By this time the Germans recognized the formidability of the Shermans when amassed in large numbers. *Voyageur Press collection*

considered complimentary, believing it would bolster the confidence of the men who rode the Sherman into harm's way.

The article related, "The German High Command maintains a museum of captured tanks—or one might say a kind of technical school where some of our most highly skilled engineers and a number of officers specially chosen for the purpose are testing those monsters. . . . These tests are carried out in a forest region of central Germany where the terrain up-hill and down-hill is intersected by ravines and all manner of depressions of the ground. The results are embodied in long tabulations not unlike those prepared by scientific laboratories, and in recommendation to the designers of German counter-weapons, who pass them on to the tank factories and armament shops. . . ."

The Germans criticize the performance of the British cruiser tank and the American Stuart light and Lee medium tanks in service with the Soviets and the British through the Lend-Lease program, labeling each of these a failure. However, the commentary on the Sherman is quite different.

"This criticism does not apply, however, to the most recent North American development, the 'General Sherman,'" the German author continues. "The latter represents one of the special accomplishments of the North American laboratories. With its turtle-shaped crown rising in one piece above the 'tub' and turret it must be regarded as quite a praiseworthy product of the North American steel industry. The first things to attract attention are serial construction and fulfillment of the almost arrogant requirements of the North American automobile industry as regards speed, smooth riding, and streamlined contour of the ensemble. It is equipped with soft rubber boots, that is with rubber padding on the individual treads of the caterpillar mechanism. It seems largely intended for a civilized landscape or, to put the matter in terms of strategy, for thoroughly cultivated areas in Tunisian Africa and for the invasion of Europe. It represents the climax of the enemy's accomplishments in this line of production."

The article concludes with a broad assessment of the Allies' intended purpose for the Sherman. "We look upon the 'General Sherman' as embodying a type of strategy that is conceived in terms of movement: it is a 'running' tank, all the more since the Americans most likely expected to use it on readily passable terrain, that is on European soil. The caliber of its principal weapon is slightly in excess of the maximum so far attained by the foreign countries. It is spacious inside. Its aeroplane motor is of light weight. It is a series product, the same as its cast-steel coat, the latter being modeled into an almost artistic-looking contour, in such manner as to offer invariably a curved, that is a deflecting surface to an approaching bullet."

In a sense, the Germans were prophetic with their appraisal of the Sherman. The tank was built for speed, sacrificing armor protection and heavier firepower in exchange for it. The Sherman was also intended for mass production, ease of maintenance, and reliability on the battlefield, while its vast numbers would be capable of overwhelming the relatively low German industrial output of PzKpfw. V Panther medium and PzKpfw. VI Tiger heavy tanks, precision weapons with substantial armor and powerful main guns that were expensive to produce and prone to mechanical breakdown.

By the end of World War II, swarms of Shermans advancing steadily eastward did simply overwhelm the opposing German armor. However, the cost was great, and the relative merits and shortcomings of the Sherman tank will be the subject of debate as long as historians continue to study warfare.

Certainly, however, the Sherman had staying power. Seventy-five years after the prototype entered its evaluation period in the United States, elderly Sherman tanks are still seen in service. From the Soviet Union to the Sinai, the Pacific to the Balkans, and the Mediterranean Basin to the hedgerows of France, the ubiquitous Sherman has compiled an incomparable service history and remains one of the most enduring and iconic weapons developed during the twentieth century.

PART I

ARMORED HERITAGE

CHAPTER ONE

Early Tank Development

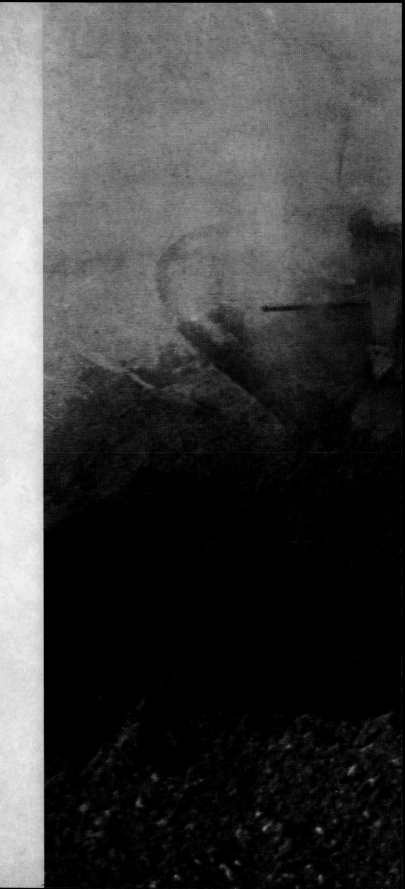

On the morning of September 15, 1916, on the stalemated Somme front during World War I, the British Army changed the course of land warfare with the deployment of forty-nine Mark I tanks. It was the first time in history that these armor-clad behemoths, armed with machine guns and cannon, entered combat.

The tanks crept forward toward their starting positions near the French towns of Flers and Courcelette, and within minutes thirteen of them had fallen away due to mechanical difficulties. Another fourteen broke down just after the signal was given to begin their assault on the German lines. Eventually, only nine were left operational, but these were enough to panic many of the enemy troops they confronted.

For the next three days, the British tanks advanced here and there, supporting the infantry and penetrating about a mile beyond the original German defensive line. Although they never concentrated in great numbers, their mere presence was enough to signal that a new era in warfare had begun. The first armored action at the Somme was in fact the validation of years of experimentation, testing, engineering, and design work by visionary, military-minded individuals in several countries.

Those ponderous, rudimentary tanks that took the field at the Somme and later during the Great War were the precursors of the spearheads that swept across Europe with speed, firepower, and armor protection a generation later during

This image of a Mark I series British tank purportedly shows the armored vehicle in combat during World War I. The tank is attempting to clear a shell hole, with its sponson-mounted cannon pointing in the direction of the enemy. *William Ivor Castle/George Grantham Bain Collection Library of Congress*

World War II, and even those modern marvels that prowl the battlefields of the new millennium.

Along the way there were milestones, and one of the most significant was the introduction of the Medium Tank M4, the Sherman that appeared in the mid-twentieth century and remained in service for decades. A few Shermans are probably still clanking along somewhere around the globe, and now seventy-five years after its introduction, the Medium Tank M4 remains an icon of the most catastrophic war in the history of mankind. The Sherman traces its lineage back to the first conceptions of armored warfare, and it was the product of half a century of technological advancement coupled with the development of tactical doctrine.

Since the earliest days of combat, the idea of the armored fighting vehicle, impervious to enemy fire, transporting combat troops in relative safety and breaking through the enemy's defenses, had fascinated inventors, conquerors, and kings. The siege engine of the Assyrians, the Greek phalanx, Hannibal's Carthaginian war elephants, and Leonardo da Vinci's circular tank of heavy wood reinforced with sheet metal preceded the experimental caterpillar-tracked "cart that carries its own road," a design of the 1770s conceived by British inventor and politician Richard Lovell Edgeworth. It was Edgeworth who realized that the caterpillar track was much more practical to facilitate cross-country movement than the standard wheel.

Opposite: A column of infantrymen follows a British tank somewhere near the front lines during World War I. This Mark I features a double-wheeled steering tail and a triangular wire mesh apparatus to deflect German grenades. The British Army changed the course of land warfare when it deployed forty-nine Mark I tanks—the first time that these armor-clad behemoths entered combat. *National Library of Scotland*

Below: A British Mark I series tank is painted in a camouflage scheme designed by Solomon Joseph Solomon, an artist and pioneer in the art of military concealment. Note the trailing wheel that helped the tank to maintain its course in rough terrain. *George Grantham Bain Collection Library of Congress*

Although these precursors to the modern tank were a diverse lot, they shared one common attribute—each was dependent for mobility on the brute strength of men or animals. During the mid-nineteenth century, the introduction of armor plating revolutionized the construction of naval vessels and war at sea. It was, therefore, not a great leap for such riveted iron protection to be applied to land vehicles. However, the problem of propulsion persisted. During the Crimean and Boer wars, the steam engine was employed on a limited basis to move artillery, but it proved impractical. The emergence of the internal combustion engine powered by petroleum-based fuel provided a breakthrough.

With the identification of the components necessary to produce a practical armored fighting vehicle, pioneer innovators set to work. For a while, though, the idea of

the tank remained fodder for science fiction as related in "The Land Ironclads," a short story written by H. G. Wells and published in the December 1903 edition of the *Strand* magazine published in Great Britain. Wells's imagination conjured up great machines that were ". . . essentially long, narrow and very strong steel frameworks carrying the engines, and borne upon eight pairs of big pedrail wheels, each about ten feet in diameter, each a driving wheel and set upon long axles free to swivel round a common axis . . . [with] look-out points at small ports all-around the upper edge of the adjustable skirt of twelve-inch iron plating which protected the whole affair. . . ."

Meanwhile, by 1900 there was more to the development of the tank than just imagination. The immediate forerunner of the tank, the armored car, was coming into its own. Most of the armored cars that

The Charron-Girardot et Voigt 1902 was an early armored car of French manufacture. The vehicle included an open gun tub with 7mm armor mounting a Hotchkiss machine gun. The vehicle demonstrates the growing emphasis on mobile military firepower in the early twentieth century. *Public Domain*

Left: A pair of British soldiers demonstrates the Hornsby Chain Tractor manufactured by R. Hornsby & Sons Ltd. The chain tractor was operated with primitive caterpillar tracks. Agricultural engineer Richard Hornsby was a pioneer in tractor development, and early tank designers borrowed extensively from his work. *Public Domain*

Middle: The German Panzerspähwagen Ehrhardt E-V/4 armored reconnaissance car presented a towering silhouette; however, it carried armor up to 9mm thick and mounted three machine guns. The vehicle entered service during World War I. *Public Domain*

Right: The Belgian army took an early interest in the development of the armored car, and with the outbreak of World War I its inventory of the vehicles was substantially higher than that of other nations. In this photo, a trio of Belgian soldiers appears to be posing for the photographer as they point their Hotchkiss machine gun toward a distant enemy. *Public Domain*

appeared in the early years of the twentieth century were conversions from civilian automobiles. Prior to World War I, the Belgian army was a pioneer in the deployment of the armored car, particularly the Minerva 38CV, a modified automobile mounting an 8mm Hotchkiss machine gun.

Early British armored car development was within the sphere of the Royal Navy, and Petty Officer L. Gutteridge introduced a design built around the Ford Model T with armor plating 5mm thick. In France, the Charron-Girardot et Voigt was unveiled in 1905. Largely the work of Russian army officer M. A. Nakasjidze, the Charron resembled a steel box with a simple turret on top. The German Panzerkraftwagen Ehrhardt BAK (Ballon Abwehr Kanone), an antiaircraft weapon, and the Austrian Austro-Daimler were also products of pre–World War I research and development in Europe.

An early American contribution to the development of the tank came from the Holt Manufacturing Company based in Stockton, California. In 1894, the company began manufacturing tractors powered by internal combustion engines paired with chassis that moved atop caterpillar tracks. Initially intended for the farming, mining, and forestry industries and other endeavors that required traction and some degree of mobility in terrain that was often muddy, steep, and difficult for a wheeled vehicle to traverse, the Holt tractors, particularly the Models 45, 75, and 120, were modified for military use.

The Holt tractors, some powered by large, six-cylinder engines, were ideal as prime movers for artillery and as recovery vehicles or for towing mobile repair, headquarters, and workshop facilities behind the front lines during World War I. By the autumn of 1916, a Holt Company executive announced that the firm had sold approximately one thousand tractors to Great Britain for use in the war effort. He added, "We have had nothing to do with putting armor on them, or placing machine guns, but some of our men at Aldershot, England, recently were notified that the British Government intended to arm some of the tractors and use them for work other than the usual towing of big guns."

Indeed, the British intended just that. In 1912, Australian Lancelot Eldin de Mole had offered a tank design to the War Office, but the idea gained little support. De Mole's work was discounted again in 1914 and 1916, but after the end of World War I he received a small measure of recognition for his contribution to British tank development. In the autumn of 1914, Lt. Col. Ernest Swinton persuaded the War Office to purchase Holt tractors for use in the field and then advocated their development into fighting machines.

With its experience in armored cars, the Royal Navy took the lead in tank development and the prototype "Big Willie," also known as "Mother," entered production as the Mark I in early 1916. The stalemate on the Western Front contributed to a quickened pace in British tank development, and

the rhombus-shaped series that followed the Mark I resulted in numerous improvements.

The Mark IV was produced in the greatest numbers and was the centerpiece of the massed British armored attack at the Battle of Cambrai fought November 20 through December 8, 1917. More than 1,200 Mark IV tanks were built during the Great War in two variants, Male and Female, the Male carrying .30-caliber machine guns and a 6-pounder gun, while the Female was armed only with machine guns.

At the same time that the British heavy tank was being tested in battle, a division of labor began to emerge with the Medium Tank Mark A, dubbed the Whippet, being deployed as a swift weapon that could exploit breaches in enemy lines. The Whippet embodied the concept of mobility. Its top speed of eight miles per hour was considerably faster than that of larger tanks of the era.

Meanwhile, Captain Levavasseur, an artillery officer in the French Army, peddled his "automobile cannon project" to anyone who would listen. Levavasseur mounted an armored box on a caterpillar-tracked chassis and placed a 75mm cannon inside. Some historians consider the project the first real attempt to develop a workable tank. Levavasseur was rebuffed several times, and the French military establishment killed his proposal for good in 1908.

Nevertheless, the coming of the Great War revived and energized French tank development, and Gen. Jean Baptiste Eugene Estienne, remembered today as the "Father of the Tank" in the French army, championed the experimentation. The inefficiency of the French military bureaucracy and a heated rivalry among manufacturing concerns resulted in two heavy tanks being developed simultaneously, and both the Schneider CA 1 and the Saint-Chamond entered production. The ponderous Schneider was twenty-one feet long and weighed fourteen tons, while the Saint-Chamond weighed twenty-three tons.

Despite such infighting that was detrimental to the war effort, the French produced the finest tank of World War I. Automaker Louis Renault, at the urging of Estienne, initiated a light tank design, and the resulting FT-17 literally broke new ground. The FT-17 included a turret with a 360-degree traverse and mounted a 37mm Puteaux SA 1918 main gun along with a pair of 8mm Hotchkiss machine guns. More than 2,700 were built, and the generation of tanks

Left: The Allies utilized the Holt Model 120 tractor in large numbers as an artillery prime mover during World War I. It featured caterpillar tracks that later became standard on armored vehicles. Later models were manufactured without the front tiller wheel. *Public Domain*

Above: French soldiers pause in the rugged Vosges Mountains of southern France during the spring of 1915. They appear to be operating a Holt artillery tractor to haul a heavy 155mm field gun into firing position. *Public Domain*

Right: Soldiers fire machine guns from their Davidson-Cadillac semi-armored antiaircraft military car, the first American military antiaircraft vehicle. The antiaircraft car was a variant of the basic armored car designed by Royal P. Davidson and produced by Cadillac in 1915. *Public Domain*

Below: Cadets of the Northwestern Military and Naval Academy stand at attention behind one of their Davidson-Cadillac armored cars during a 1915 convoy from Chicago to San Francisco. The school's commandant, Royal P. Davidson, led the convoy and designed the vehicle that was later produced by Cadillac. *Public Domain*

that were manufactured during the years between the world wars bore an unmistakable resemblance to Renault's design.

Although German engineers had experimented with tanks as early as 1911, the appearance of the British Mark I at the Somme spurred the Kaiser's military to action. Several heavy and light tank prototypes were considered by 1917, but the only German tank to enter production and reach the battlefield was the Panzerkampfwagen A7V, a massive iron box stretching twenty-six feet long with a crew of eighteen soldiers. Armed with a 57mm Maxim-Nordenfelt main weapon and six or more 7.92mm Maxim MG08 machine guns, the A7V was unwieldy and suffered from numerous design faults. Crewmen were often overcome by the tank's engine exhaust fumes. Only twenty examples of the A7V were completed before the end of World War I.

Although Imperial Russia was wracked by civil unrest and soon to be in the throes of the Bolshevik Revolution, twenty-three-year-old aircraft designer and engineer Aleksandr Porokhovschikov conceived plans for the Vezdekhod, a small oval-shaped armored vehicle that weighed only 3.5 tons. A two-man crew operated the Vezdekhod, which was armed with a single machine gun. In sharp contrast, chemist and inventor Dmitri Mendeleev worked on a mammoth design of 170 tons, crewed by eight soldiers and mounting a 120mm cannon. Army Lt. Nikolai Lebedenko came up with the Czar Tank, which looked more like a carriage than a machine of war, and another project simply known as the 20-Ton Tank was stopped cold by the Revolution of 1917.

While the primary American contribution to the development of the tank in the early twentieth century was the Holt tractor and its proven caterpillar system, there were stirrings of inventiveness. Around 1900, Royal Page Davidson, an army officer and later the commandant of the Northwestern Military Academy in Highland Park, Illinois, modified a Duryea Tricar, one of the models built in limited

numbers by pioneer automobile manufacturer Charles Duryea. The Tricar was powered by a six-horsepower engine, and Davidson added a 7mm Colt machine gun and a shield for the driver and machine gun operator. He also experimented with machine guns mounted on a pair of steam-powered cars built by his cadets at the military academy.

From 1909 to 1912, Davidson purchased at least three Cadillac automobiles, converting one to carry a tripod-mounted machine gun and two others specifically to destroy observation balloons. By 1915, he had designed five Cadillac cars with machine guns for military use, and the Davidson-Cadillac armored car became the first purpose-built armored vehicle completed in the United States.

At the same time that Davidson's armored car was being tested, relatively obscure American efforts to develop a rudimentary tank took place. Among the earliest known such vehicles built by 1915 were the Shaffer Armoured Tractor, constructed on the chassis of a Fageol Motors tractor that was originally used in the fruit cultivation industry, and the Automatic Land Cruisers I and II, built on the frame of the Automatic Machine Company's Alligator tractor, which ran on nineteen bogey wheels. The first of these mounted a Driggs-Schroeder 1-pounder gun in the bow while the commander sat on a raised seat beneath a centered cupola. The Automatic Land Cruiser II differed with rounded armor plating, the addition of four machine guns, and an arrangement of six clusters with three bogeys each.

Although these early efforts were indeed innovative, they failed to garner enough support within the

Above: British Maj. Gen. Sir Ernest Dunlop Swinton was instrumental in the development of the tank during World War I. Swinton observed the use of artillery tractors and wrote of the possibility that their design could contribute to the fielding of an armored fighting vehicle. He is also credited with coining the term "tank." *Public Domain*

Top left: A British Mark V Male tank sits idle on a desolate battlefield somewhere in France. The Mark V Male featured sponson-mounted 57mm guns and four 7.7mm Hotchkiss machine guns; the Female variant was armed with six machine guns. *Public Domain*

In the spring of 1918, the British introduced the Medium Mark A Whippet tank to combat in Flanders. With a top speed of just over eight miles per hour and an armament of four 7.7mm Hotchkiss machine guns, it provided something of a speed advantage over other tanks. This photo demonstrates its remarkable service life, depicting Japanese soldiers operating Whippets in Manchuria in the 1930s. *Public Domain*

US military to gain real traction. With the outbreak of the Great War, the US Army lagged behind the European powers in the development of tanks, and as a result the American Expeditionary Force (AEF) was obliged to purchase tanks from its allies, principally the French Renault FT-17.

The US Army Tank Corps was established in France under the auspices of the AEF in the winter of 1917 to 1918, while the Tank Service was formed in the United States in March 1918. Two of the army's most prominent future officers became early leaders within these organizations. Captain Dwight D. Eisenhower was assigned to the 65th Engineer Regiment at Camp Meade, Maryland, in February 1918 with orders to

turn his command into the 1st Battalion, Heavy Tank Service. He was later promoted to the temporary rank of lieutenant colonel and given his first independent command at Camp Colt, the primary training facility for the Tank Corps, near Gettysburg, Pennsylvania. Lieutenant Colonel George S. Patton Jr. organized the Army Tank School at Langres, France, in early 1918 and led the 304th Tank Brigade in action at the St. Mihiel Salient and in the Meuse-Argonne Offensive.

Eisenhower went on to attain the rank of five-star general of the army, led the Allies to victory in Western Europe during World War II, and served two terms as president of the United States. Patton rose to the rank of four-star general and became one of the

Top left: A French tank soldier sits with his legs down the open hatch of his Renault FT-17, nicknamed the "Tiger." This tank may be forming up for a military review or parade. More than three thousand examples of the influential tank were produced by French industry, and nearly one thousand more were manufactured in the United States. *Public Domain*

Above: A French Schneider CA1 tank maneuvers carefully on a crowded street during World War I. Along with the Saint-Chamond, the Schneider was one of two rival tank designs to which the French military establishment contributed substantial resources during the Great War. The Schneider was unwieldy in battle but packed a significant punch with its 75mm gun and two Hotchkiss machine guns. *Public Domain*

Left: Renault FT-17 tanks parade through the Arc de Triomphe and down the Champs-Élysées in Paris as soldiers salute and civilians look on. The French FT-17 was perhaps the most advanced tank design to emanate from World War I. Its appearance presages the more formidable armored vehicles that would do battle in Europe a generation later during World War II. *Public Domain*

most revered and controversial commanders in the history of the US Army. He gained lasting fame in command of the Third Army during World War II.

The first tank to enter production in the United States was the M1917 light tank, a license-built copy of the French Renault FT-17. Approximately 950 were produced, but fewer than a dozen reached the battlefields of Europe before the Armistice ended World War I. Another foray into tank design and production ended in failure as the Holt Gas-Electric Tank never proceeded beyond the prototype stage.

The first tank that was both designed and built in the United States was the Ford Model 1918, conceived in anticipation of a shortage of the Renault FT-17. The Model 1918 weighed three tons and mounted a single .30-caliber Browning machine gun. Although the army contracted for fifteen thousand, only fifteen were completed by the end of the war.

The Mark VIII or Liberty Tank was the first heavy tank to enter production in the United States. Initially a joint design effort between the British and Americans, the Mark VIII was intended to spearhead a massive offensive against the Germans on the Western Front scheduled for 1919. That offensive, of course, never took place. Only 125 Mark VIII tanks were completed from 1918 to 1920, and some of these served with the army into the 1930s.

Although the command establishment of the US Army could not completely ignore the implications of mechanization on the modern battlefield observed during World War I, there was little continuing support for a real commitment to the development of an armored force, let alone a doctrine that would guide the tank's use during conflicts to come. As a result, during the years between the world wars, the US Army fell behind those of other industrialized nations in the development and deployment of the tank as a weapon of war.

Ironically, a generation later, as the Allied nations were locked with the Axis in the death struggle of World War II, the United States would demonstrate its industrial prowess with the production of nearly fifty thousand M4 Sherman medium tanks.

Above: A large group of French officers and soldiers gathers around a Renault FT-17 tank on a hillside. The FT-17 was the world's first tank to carry its main armament in a fully rotating turret. In the case of the FT-17, this was either a 37mm Puteaux SA 18 gun or an 8mm Hotchkiss machine gun. *Public Domain*

Right: British soldiers ride atop a Mark IV tank as it traverses a steep incline. The Mark IV was produced from May 1917 through the end of World War I, with more than 1,200 completed. It offered some improvements over earlier tank models, including better armor protection and a more optimal relocation of the fuel tank. *Public Domain*

Young George Patton in Combat

On September 12, 1918, Lt. Col. George S. Patton Jr. planned and led American troops and tanks in the US Army's first documented wartime armored action. Accompanied by French tank units, elements of the US 304th Tank Brigade advanced in support of the 1st and 42nd Infantry Divisions during the fighting at St. Mihiel.

During the day's action, Patton reportedly met Brig. Gen. Douglas MacArthur on the battlefield, led his tanks across a bridge that had potentially been mined by the Germans, and placed himself directly in harm's way for most of the time his unit was engaged. Rather than remaining safely in the rear to direct the advance, Patton preferred to lead from the front and was firmly reprimanded for actually outdistancing his advancing tanks and being out of communication with higher levels of command for an extended period.

Patton's display of bravado presaged his later exploits and endeared him to his men. He also absorbed valuable lessons, including the fact that tanks advancing across muddy ground consume fuel at a higher rate than those traversing dry terrain. Interestingly, prior to the action the far-sighted Patton had personally developed a towed sled that was designed to carry fuel to tanks in forward areas.

Two weeks later, Patton and his armor were again in action. On September 26, he led his command in the Meuse-Argonne sector. Remembering the earlier rebuke, Patton devised a system of homing pigeons and runners that could convey messages to his superior officers, keeping them informed of the progress of the advance and allowing him to remain close to the action.

The fighting in support of the 28th and 35th Infantry Divisions was intense and prolonged. As he directed tanks and troops forward, Patton again found himself outdistancing his command. This time he was only about forty yards from German machine gun positions. A bullet slammed into his leg, and his orderly pulled him to the safety of a shell hole. Although he nearly lost his life in the process, the young officer continued to direct his tanks forward, and twenty-five German machine gun positions were destroyed. However, Patton's brigade was a spent force, suffering nearly

In 1918, a young George S. Patton Jr. stands before a French Renault FT-17 tank in service with the US Army. Patton was one of the first American officers to urge the army to develop armored fighting vehicles and was so vocal that he was nearly court-martialed. During World War II, General Patton became legendary as the commander of the Third Army and a hard-driving tank soldier. *National Archives*

ninety percent casualties in two weeks of combat and losing virtually all of its tanks.

While recuperating from his wound in a field hospital, Patton learned that he had been promoted to full colonel. He was later awarded the Distinguished Service Cross for his valor. When World War I ended, Patton was one of only a few US Army officers with combat experience in tanks. The knowledge gained served him well a quarter-century later during World War II.

Right: A prototype of the Mark VIII "Liberty," the first heavy tank to enter production in the United States, undergoes testing in 1918. The tank was intended to spearhead an offensive that never happened, and only 125 Liberties were built. *US Army*

Below: In the summer of 1938, an armored tractor ploughs a field at the kibbutz Mishmar HaEmek in Palestine, later northern Israel. Note the steel helmet that one of the operators is wearing. The tractor itself is indicative of the advances in armor protection that were made during the interwar years. *Public Domain*

CHAPTER TWO

US Armored Doctrine

The long and winding road to the debut of the M4 Sherman was shaped by several external factors. In the post–World War I United States the availability of a relative few operational tanks, a policy of fiscal austerity as it related to the military, and the prevailing view among senior army commanders that tanks should be subordinate to the infantry retarded both the development of the tank itself and the doctrine for its use in modern warfare.

The US Army underwent an extensive reorganization soon after World War I ended, and Gen. John J. Pershing, commander of the American Expeditionary Force in Europe during the Great War, was one of many senior officers who were convinced that the primary role of the tank in battle was to provide direct fire support to the infantry. Therefore, he testified in 1919 before the joint US Senate and House of Representatives Committee on Military Affairs that the tank should be subordinated to the infantry branch.

In the wake of Pershing's testimony, the resulting National Defense Act of 1920 mandated that the Tank Corps be disbanded and its units reassigned to infantry formations. The postwar reduction of the standing army left only two heavy tank battalions and four light battalions in service.

After World War I, Dwight Eisenhower returned to Camp Meade and the Tank Corps. George S. Patton Jr. was also posted there. The two officers became fast friends and spent hours riding around the Maryland

Fitters are hard at work assembling an American-made M2A4 light tank that has just arrived at an ordnance depot in Great Britain via Lend-Lease in 1941. The M2 was a fine light tank, well suited for reconnaissance but lacking in armor protection and firepower in tank-versus-tank encounters. Nevertheless, along with the M3, it would be a significant step toward the development of the M4. Note the name that has been applied to the turret. *National Archives*

countryside discussing armored tactics and the use of massed formations of tanks as weapons of decision, exploiting a breakthrough of enemy lines and rapidly advancing into rear areas to disrupt enemy troop concentrations, command structure, and lines of supply. Eisenhower and Patton were quite vocal in their advocacy of the tank, and the two were threatened with court martial when they refused to tone down their rhetoric.

In April 1922, the War Department issued a policy statement that further restricted the study and development of tanks and their battlefield doctrine. It plainly stated that the primary role of the tank was "to facilitate the uninterrupted advance of the riflemen in the attack."

By the late 1920s, however, two significant events occurred that changed the course of mechanization in the US Army. In 1928, Secretary of War Dwight F. Davis attended a series of maneuvers and demonstrations conducted by the British Army's Experimental Armored Force. He left the maneuvers with a revised perspective on the tank and the embryonic but vocal movement to mechanize the US military. Davis ordered the creation of a mechanized force for

demonstration and evaluation, including combined arms elements with infantry, artillery, cavalry, and air assets contributing to the study and discourse. Although budgetary constraints and the lack of serviceable equipment curtailed Davis's experiment by 1929, the results were encouraging enough for the War Department Mechanization Board to recommend the further mechanization of the military.

At the same time, Lt. Col. Adna R. Chaffee Jr., a former cavalry officer, was taking notice of the development of tanks and armored doctrine in other countries. Chaffee, alarmed by what he believed was a lack of vision on the part of senior army officers, was a planning officer with the War Department General Staff in 1927. He transferred to the post of executive officer with the 1st Cavalry Regiment, one of the few mechanized formations in the army at the time, and then returned to the War Department in 1934 as the chief of the budget and planning branch, where he was influential in securing financial appropriations for the development of tanks and revitalizing the discussion of armored doctrine among senior officers.

By 1930, Gen. Douglas MacArthur had become army chief of staff. Despite the fact that the

Experimental Mechanized Force had been disbanded a year earlier, he acknowledged the need for continuing mechanization. Confronted with a lack of funding, MacArthur made the difficult choice to retain personnel in the active army rather than enact manpower cuts in favor of spending limited resources on the development of tanks and other motorized vehicles.

Nevertheless, in 1931 MacArthur pronounced, "The horse has no higher degree of mobility today than he had a thousand years ago. The time has therefore arrived when the Cavalry arm must either replace or assist the horse as a means of transportation, or else pass into the limbo of discarded formations."

Meanwhile, visionary officers in European armies began to grasp the potential of the tank as an offensive weapon in its own right, while the development of the tank continued within the financial constraints of the Great Depression and the

Above: American troops in French FT-17 tanks advance to the frontline in the Argonnes Forest in September 1918. Dwight Eisenhower became familiar with the FT-17 while training armored troops at Camp Colt, Pennsylvania, and Camp Meade, Maryland. *National Archives*

Right: Two soldiers of the US Army's 301st Heavy Tank Battalion pose with a log mockup at Camp Meade prior to departure for England and intense training on actual British-made Mark V tanks. This photo was taken circa 1917. *Public Domain*

The Father of the Armored Force

Lieutenant Colonel Adna R. Chaffee Jr., the officer who was instrumental in securing the financial resources necessary for continuing research and development of armored fighting vehicles in the US Army amid the austerity of the 1930s, is remembered as the "Father of the Armored Force."

At the request of Army Chief of Staff Gen. George C. Marshall, Chaffee attended a meeting at the War Department on June 10, 1940, to discuss the formation of an Armored Force, which had been vigorously opposed by the chiefs of both the cavalry and infantry branches of the army command structure. His eloquent and powerful address to the gathering of influential officers made the case for modernization.

Chaffee, a 1906 graduate of the US Military Academy who attained the rank of major general during his career, commented in part, "We have a directive to consider the organization of two armored divisions and how we can get them—and speed is essential. We have got to do it now. That means that we must make use, in starting the organization of these two divisions, of what we have and go forward from that as the material comes in. Cavalry contributes everything it has; infantry everything it has. We must not stop and haggle over a lot of details and figure out a lot of things that have been studied over and over again by boards and commanding officers in the field and tested in maneuvers time and again. . . ."

When the War Department authorized the establishment of the Armored Force a month later, Chaffee was placed in command and became the catalyst for the integration of mechanized forces from the infantry and cavalry branches into the modern military organization that proved essential to the later Allied victory in World War II. He was also largely responsible for the formation of the 1st and 2nd Armored Divisions, the first of their kind in the US Army.

Although his influence was profound and the Armored Force came into existence with greater efficiency because of his efforts, Chaffee did not live to see the object of his advocacy prove itself in wartime. He died of cancer on August 22, 1941, four months before the United States entered World War II.

---

inevitable bureaucratic entanglements that influenced both the evolution of the machine and its gradually maturing doctrine. In Great Britain, Maj. Gen. J. F. C. Fuller had conceived the massive thrust of tanks at Cambrai during World War I and championed the idea of the armored spearhead that would smash through the enemy line—followed by light tanks and motorized infantry to exploit the breakthrough.

Captain B. H. Liddell-Hart, a former British Army officer, advocated his Expanding Torrent Theory. Liddell-Hart compared a military offensive to rushing water and saw the tank as a breakthrough weapon that would thrust deeply behind enemy lines, flooding rear areas with powerful, fast-moving forces.

By the time Adolf Hitler openly repudiated the Treaty of Versailles in March 1935 and unveiled the extent of German rearmament to the world, the early PzKpfw. I and II tanks were already in production, heralding a steady progression of heavier armored vehicles and populating the ranks of the Wehrmacht panzer divisions that swiftly conquered Poland in 1939 and shattered French resistance within weeks in the spring of 1940.

German General Heinz Guderian, probably influenced by Fuller and Liddell-Hart, is known as the father of the combined arms doctrine referred to as "Blitzkrieg." As German armored spearheads breached enemy lines, tanks and motorized infantry slashed into the enemy rear, artillery pounded troop concentrations, and dive bombers acted as flying artillery to hit routes of advance, communications, and logistics infrastructure.

Opposite: Young US Army Tank Corps officers George S. Patton Jr. (circled left) and Dwight Eisenhower (circled right) pose with other personnel of the fledgling armored forces, probably at Camp Meade in the early 1920s. Patton and Eisenhower, both strong advocates of the tank in warfare, became close friends during their days at Camp Meade and of course went on to lasting fame in World War II. *Public Domain*

Above: In 1928, US Secretary of War Dwight F. Davis attended a series of demonstrations in England conducted by the British Army's Experimental Armored Force. Impressed with what he saw, Davis ordered the formation of armored units in the US Army. *Public Domain*

Right: Brigadier General Adna R. Chaffee sits at his desk at a military post during the 1930s. Chaffee was one of the earliest advocates of the use of armor in the US Army. He predicted a steadily increasing role for mechanized forces during future wars and is considered to be the father of the armored forces of the army. Chaffee did not live to see tanks deployed in great numbers during wartime. He died in August 1941, months before the US entry into World War II. *National Archives*

Opposite: A pair of French-designed Renault FT-17 tanks purchased from France sit ready for training exercises at Camp Meade in 1921. The six-ton Renault was also manufactured under license in the United States and was a mainstay of the early US armored forces due to a lag in American tank development. *Public Domain*

In France, Lt. Col. Charles de Gaulle, who rose to lead his country's fight against the Nazis during World War II, was a vociferous advocate of armored forces, so much so that he earned the nickname "Colonel Motor" and enraged so many senior officers of the French army that he was nearly cashiered. France produced the Char B1 bis, perhaps the finest tank to emerge from the interwar period.

However, the flaw in French tactics that was laid bare with the German onslaught of 1940 was the simple fact that French tanks were tied to infantry formations and committed to battle piecemeal rather than in concentrated armored formations. Thus, the

French tactical doctrine was similar to that of the US Army, relegating the tank to the infantry support role and negating its potentially decisive firepower when deployed en masse.

Soviet Red Army officers Mikhail Tukhachevsky and Vladimir Triandafillov advocated the Deep Penetration or Deep Battle Theory, applying continuous pressure along a broad front until a breakthrough was achieved and followed with the deployment of the three hundred thousand troops and 2,800 tanks of the shock army to exploit the breach.

Throughout the 1930s, the War Department wrestled with mechanization, issuing periodic directives and revisions to its policy. In 1938, a restatement of that policy addressed the intended use of both mechanized cavalry and the infantry tank force, resulting in two different paths toward doctrinal maturity. The mechanized cavalry was intended for reconnaissance along with far-ranging and independent movement, while the tank continued in a subordinate role with the infantry and was to operate in close coordination as a support weapon.

In the same year Maj. Gen. John K. Herr, the chief of the army's Cavalry Branch, maintained his archaic position in the face of mounting evidence that the dependence of the modern military upon the horse was rapidly waning. "We must not be misled to our own detriment to assume that the untried machine can displace the proved and tried horse," Herr declared. He later asserted that the horse could "live off the land" while the machine could not and that the noble beast had "stood the acid test of war."

During the two decades that elapsed between the world wars, little changed regarding the use of tanks in the US Army. Accepted doctrine stated, "As a rule, tanks are employed to assist the advance of infantry foot troops, either preceding or accompanying the infantry assault echelon."

As mechanization began to creep forward in the early 1930s, it became necessary to obey the conditions of the National Defense Act of 1920 to the letter. Armored vehicles classified as "tanks" would

Above: German Gen. Heinz Guderian was an early advocate of the development of the tank in the Wehrmacht. He led German armored forces to several victories early in World War II and fell in and out of favor with Hitler during the course of the conflict. Guderian is also considered by some to be the "Father of the Blitzkrieg." *Public Domain*

Left: Captain B. H. Liddell-Hart, a former British Army officer, developed an influential offensive doctrine known as the "Expanding Torrent Theory." His ideas compared offensive military action to the motion of rushing water and included the tank as a prime weapon of breakthrough and pursuit. *Public Domain*

The French-built Char B1 bis heavy tank was among the best armored fighting vehicles of its kind during the early days of World War II. However, its firepower and combat capability were squandered due to the flawed tactics of the French Army's senior commanders. Here, a German soldier sits atop a disabled Char B1 somewhere in France. *Public Domain*

Opposite: American engineer J. Walter Christie was a pioneer in the development of operational armored vehicles. This Christie tank prototype was photographed during trials in the United States in the mid-1930s. Christie was best known for his innovative suspension system, and his design work was well received in the Soviet Union during the interwar years. *Harris & Ewing Collection/Library of Congress*

Left: Soviet Marshal Mikhail Tukhachevsky developed the "Deep Penetration," or "Deep Battle" theory along with Gen. Vladimir Triandafillov, in which they advocated continuous pressure against enemy lines along a broad front until a breakthrough could be affected and exploited by massed troops and tanks. Tukhachevsky was later executed during Josef Stalin's purge of the Red Army senior command structure during the 1930s. Triandafillov died in a plane crash in 1931. *Public Domain*

Right: General Charles de Gaulle led the Free French forces during World War II. As a young officer he was among the foremost proponents of tank development and tactics during the interwar years. De Gaulle earned the nickname "Colonel Motor" and led French tanks against the Germans in the spring of 1940. *Library of Congress*

remain subordinate to the infantry for a time, while those armored vehicles that entered service with the mechanized cavalry were referred to as "combat cars"—virtually the same vehicles known by different names.

The evolution of the M4 Sherman tank began shortly after World War I as the armored vehicles of the Great War were evaluated and experimentation resulted in War Department guidance that two types of tanks, light and medium, should be adequate for the functions that armor was intended to perform on the battlefield. The specifications for the light tank included a weight not to exceed five tons and that it should be transportable by truck. The medium tank was to weigh no more than fifteen tons so that it could be carried on rail cars and traverse bridges.

Producing tanks that met these specifications proved to be a struggle. Throughout the 1920s, the army sought designs that would serve the dual purposes of the cavalry and infantry support missions. The fifteen-ton M1924 failed to deliver, and though the development of a heavier twenty-three-ton tank had been authorized by

the middle of the decade, emphasis remained on the concept of the light fifteen-ton tank with the notion that it might be adequate for both purposes.

American engineer J. Walter Christie pioneered tank development and perfected a suspension system that allowed great cross country and road speeds in several prototype designs. However, each of these exceeded some weight or size specification, precluding it from acceptance by the army. Even the Ordnance Department's own prototypes did not pass muster. Eventually, Christie's suspension and other aspects of his design philosophy found receptive audiences with the military establishments of other nations, particularly the Soviet Union. Christie's influence was largely responsible for the high performance of early Soviet tanks, particularly the legendary T-34 medium tank, and in the end US

Left: Workmen repair a Soviet T-34 medium tank in a shop located in the Russian city of Chelyabinsk. The T-34 design was heavily influenced by the work of American engineer J. Walter Christie, and more examples of the tank were built than any other vehicle of its kind during World War II. *Tass/UIG/Bridgeman Collection*

Opposite: The dome of the US capitol looms in the background as an M2A3 light tank participates in Army Day parade activities on April 6, 1939. The tank's 37mm weapon and .50-caliber machine gun are prominently visible, while the suspension system resembles that of the later M4 Sherman medium tank series. *Harris & Ewing Collection/Library of Congress*

designs came to incorporate much of his innovative work as well.

On July 10, 1940, two months after German tanks smashed across the frontier of France and dashed to the English Channel, the War Department authorized the formation of the Armored Force. Its directive was issued in response to the dazzling success of the German Blitzkrieg in Poland and Western Europe. The organization of the armored division was adopted and modeled substantially after that of the German panzer division.

However, only twenty-eight new tanks—ten light and eighteen medium—were available to the US Army in the spring of 1940. On the eve of World War II, the army possessed fewer than one thousand tanks. More than nine hundred of these were obsolete.

As American industry geared up for the nation's potential entry into World War II and to supply the needs of Great Britain and other Allied nations through Lend-Lease, its limited experience in manufacturing armored vehicles had produced two primary tanks, the M2 light tank that weighed slightly less than twelve tons and mounted a 37mm main weapon along with .30- and .50-caliber machine guns, and the 20.5-ton M2 medium tank, which also mounted a 37mm main weapon and .30-caliber machine guns. Production of the M2 medium tank was, in fact, halted in the summer of 1941.

Concurrent with the realization that modern warfare required improved American tank designs and the concrete evidence of the German armored successes in both the East and West during the

early months of World War II, the War Department published Field Manual 100-5 on May 22, 1941, redefining the role of the US Army's tanks in combat.

It read in part, "The armored division is the basic large armored unit of the combined arms. It comprises troops of the essential arms and services so organized and equipped as to make it tactically and administratively a self-contained unit, capable to a considerable extent of independent action.

"The armored division is a powerfully armed and armored, highly mobile force. Its outstanding characteristics are its battlefield mobility and its protected fire power. Other important characteristics are: extended radius of action; shock power; logistical self-containment; and great sensitiveness to obstacles, unfavorable terrain, darkness and weather.

"The armored division is organized primarily to perform missions that require great mobility and firepower. It is given decisive missions. It is capable of engaging in all forms of combat, but its primary role is in offensive operations against hostile rear areas."

Field Manual 100-5 further placed tank regiments in the offensive, or "striking," echelon of the armored division and the accompanying motorized infantry in the "support" echelon, effectively reversing their earlier roles. Therefore, the tanks that were designed, manufactured, and deployed by the United States beginning in the months preceding the nation's entry into World War II were intended primarily for swift offensive operations.

Tank versus tank encounters were considered secondary from a doctrinal standpoint, and the primary responsibility for destroying enemy tanks resided with antitank guns and later with the fast, open-turreted tank destroyers developed during World War II. Light and medium tanks were best suited for rapid movement, and senior army commanders tended to discount the need for heavy tanks.

Chief among the proponents of light and medium tanks was Lt. Gen. Lesley McNair, commander of

The American-built M3 medium tank helped to even the odds against German tanks when it was supplied to British forces in the North African desert in quantity through Lend-Lease. However, its performance was limited, since its heaviest weapon—a 75mm gun—was mounted in a hull sponson with limited traverse. Its high silhouette also provided a prominent target. *US Army*

Army Ground Forces. McNair believed that the tank destroyer was capable of dealing with enemy armor, and during the war a so-called "Tank Destroyer Doctrine" emanated from this assertion. At the same time, Field Manual 17-10, ARMORED FORCE FIELD MANUAL, TACTICS AND TECHNIQUE, published on March 7, 1942, three months after US entry into World War II, echoed the philosophical transition of the army's tank doctrine.

Field Manual 17-10 stated, "The role of the Armored Force and its components is the conduct of highly mobile ground warfare, primarily offensive in character, by self-sustaining units of great power and mobility, composed of specially equipped troops of the required arms and services. Combat elements of the Armored Force operate in close cooperation with combat aviation and with large units of ground troops in the accomplishment of a mission."

Practical experience in World War II revealed that the offensive strike capability of the tank was indeed essential. However, tank versus tank combat was inevitable, and the role of infantry support was often indispensable, particularly in the reduction of enemy strongpoints that impeded the advance of ground troops. One unfortunate consequence of the emphasis on the tank's strike capability as defined in army doctrine was a pronounced delay in the development of heavy tanks by the US military.

In retrospect, the design and combat capabilities of the M4 Sherman tank would seem ideally suited for the primary role envisioned in 1941. While Nazi Germany developed heavier tanks such as the PzKpfw. V Panther and PzKpfw. VI Tiger with high-velocity 75mm and 88mm guns, the response from Allied armament designers was first to upgun the Sherman with more powerful main weapons—but such an effort took time. Meanwhile, the Sherman's initial 75mm gun and relatively thin armor were inadequate in direct combat with the latest generation of German tanks, a role for which the M4 Medium Tank was, frankly, never intended.

With the profound influence of armored doctrine dictating design and manufacturing priorities, the die was eventually cast with the M4 as the primary tank of the Western Allied forces during World War II. In time, the hard lessons of combat would starkly reveal both its strengths and weaknesses.

The exigencies of war quickened the pace of US tank development substantially, and by August 1941 the M3 medium tank, the immediate predecessor of the M4, had entered production. Both the M3 and the M4 incorporated numerous design elements of the discontinued M2 medium tank.

An M3 Grant tank, the forerunner of the M4 Sherman, raises a cloud of dust during maneuvers early in World War II. The tank's 37mm weapon has been removed temporarily, and the 75mm sponson mount is readily visible. The M3 was a stopgap tank produced until the M4, with a 75mm gun mounted in a fully traversing turret, was ready for production lines. *Office of War Information/Library of Congress*

PART II
EVOLUTION
OF AN ICON

CHAPTER THREE

The Sherman Design

The M4 Sherman tank evolved from the US Army's limited combat experience during the Great War, its observance of the armored vehicles of other armies in action, and the continuing refinement of tank designs and their combat capabilities that occurred between the world wars despite the financial constraints of the Great Depression, political infighting among military establishments, and disagreements over the most advantageous tactical deployment of the new armored weapon.

By the late 1920s, the US military had begun experimenting with tank designs that resembled the earliest of armored vehicles that were deployed two decades later during World War II. The Medium Tank M4 was the direct descendent of earlier medium and light tank models developed in the United States; however, these were never produced in great numbers. In fact, US tank production did not reach remarkable levels until the demands of World War II required the volume necessary to equip the army's own armored divisions and supply tanks to the Allied nations confronting the Nazi juggernaut in North Africa and on the Eastern Front.

On August 31, 1940, a full year after World War II had begun in Europe, the US Army Ordnance Board presented the design of the T6 medium tank as a potential replacement for the M3 medium tank, itself a relatively new design that was slated to enter production later that year. On April 18, 1941, the

This mud-spattered but newly built M4 Sherman tank, photographed after thorough evaluation at the Aberdeen Proving Grounds in Maryland, is soon to be loaded on a railroad car and then a transport vessel for the voyage to a European battlefield. *US Office of War Information/Library of Congress*

US Army's Armored Forces Board chose the T6 from among five competing designs. Specifications were finalized that September, and the T6 was completed at Aberdeen Proving Ground in Maryland, where it was also evaluated in trials. While the T6, which eventually entered production as the Medium Tank M4, was on its way toward approval, the M3 was nearing initial production as a stopgap measure.

As late as 1939, the primary medium tank in service with the US Army was the M2, a ponderous tank with a high silhouette that became obsolete almost simultaneously with the beginning of its short production run. Based on an enlargement of the M2 light tank that had been in production since the mid-1930s, the M2 medium tank stood nine feet three inches tall. Powered by a Wright Continental R975 EC2 air-cooled radial engine, it was capable of a top speed of twenty-six miles per hour. Originally known as the Wright Whirlwind, the R975 was one of a series of nine-cylinder radial engines developed by the Wright Aeronautical Division of Curtiss-Wright Corporation that was built under license and originally intended for the aircraft industry. The performance of German tanks during the early months of World War II made it readily apparent to the US military that the M2 medium tank was inadequate, and only eighteen of the original model and ninety-four of the somewhat modified M2A1 were completed.

Meanwhile, Great Britain urgently needed tanks to make good its losses in the Battle of France and its ongoing fight with the Axis in the North African desert. Time was of the essence if the United States was going to fulfill its role as President Franklin D. Roosevelt's "Arsenal of Democracy." In late 1941, the British had requested the delivery of 3,650 American medium tanks as soon as possible. In an effort to both accommodate the British and to produce a better quality tank for the new armored divisions of the

Below and opposite: During field trials at a manufacturing facility in the United States, a T6 pilot model or early-model M4 Sherman crests a steep slope as part of its mobility testing. This tank carries the shorter M2 75mm cannon, while most production Shermans sported the longer M3 75mm cannon. This is a sign of a T6 prototype or an early-production model. Early American tank designers were obsessed with extra machine guns, and this tank carries three of them mounted in the hull. Field testing proved the two center guns were extraneous, and they were removed from the design early in the production run. *William M. Rittase/US Office of War Information/Library of Congress*

PART II : EVOLUTION OF AN ICON

US Army while American engineers worked feverishly to bring a tank that could compete with the best German armor from the drawing board to the assembly line, the M3 was born.

To say that the M3 medium tank was a wartime expedient might be a bit of an understatement. Although it was obvious that the M2 was lacking, many of its components were incorporated into the M3, including the basic high-silhouetted hull, the vertical volute spring suspension, and the Wright Continental R975 engine. Later production models were powered by the General Motors 6046 diesel engine, actually a combination of two GM 6-71 engines and a Chrysler A57 engine. As many as seven soldiers crewed the tank.

The redesign that produced the M3 began in July 1940, and the new interim tank entered production

in August 1941. The most noticeable alteration to the early M2 design was the addition of a powerful 75mm M2 or M3 gun mounted in a sponson on the right side of the hull.

While the sponson mount harkened back to the days of Great War design, it was installed due to necessity. At the time the M3 entered production, there was no turret large enough or available in quantity that could accommodate a heavier weapon than the 37mm gun. However, more firepower was desperately needed as the Germans upgunned their PzKpfw. III and PzKpfw. IV tanks with high-velocity 50mm and 75mm weapons.

The British welcomed the M3 and gave it the nickname "General Lee," after Confederate Civil War Gen. Robert E. Lee. They modified some of their M3s by eliminating a small commander's cupola and lengthening the diminutive turret, which mounted a 37mm M6 gun, to accommodate radio equipment. The British dubbed these modified M3s the "General Grant," after Union Civil War Gen. Ulysses S. Grant.

The M3 Lee/Grant tank was heavily armed with its two cannon and up to four .30-caliber Browning M1919A4 machine guns. The 75mm weapon proved to be a nasty surprise for the Germans when it was first encountered in the desert, and the British and later the Americans coped with the tank's shortcomings as best they could. The most glaring of these was the fact that the sponson's traverse was limited to thirty degrees; therefore, the tank was often required to reorient itself completely during the heat of combat in order to bring the gun to bear. The Lee/Grant's high silhouette provided an easy target for enemy gunners, particularly when outlined against the sun or exposed on high ground. In addition, the tank was slow in cross-country movement with a top speed of only sixteen miles per hour, while its riveted hull was susceptible to the impact of a shell that in turn fractured the rivets and sent lethal pieces of them flying through the crew compartment like bullets.

Despite its drawbacks, the M3 Lee/Grant served its purpose. By the time production ceased in December 1942, a total of 6,258 had been completed. Many of

these were built at the Baldwin Locomotive Works in Philadelphia, Pennsylvania, and the bulk were purchased by the British. The Soviet Red Army placed a relative few in service, and the tank was immensely unpopular, receiving the dismal nickname "Coffin for Seven Brothers."

Even as the production of the Lee/Grant tank reached its greatest output, the M4 began rolling off the assembly lines of American factories, and

for a few months the two medium tank models were in production at the same time. The early history of the M4, which those tankers of the British Army who were the first to receive and operate in combat summarily nicknamed "General Sherman" after Civil War Gen. William Tecumseh Sherman, reveals that the pressing need for more and better tanks to confront the steadily improving German panzers continued unabated.

Once classified, this early artist's rendering of an M4 Sherman tank prototype presents the classic lines and easily recognizable silhouette of the tank that overwhelmed German forces in Western Europe with sheer weight of numbers, earning credit as a weapon that helped to win the final victory for the Allies in World War II. *US Army*

The Vertical Volute Spring Suspension

One of the key design features in the early variants of the M4 Sherman medium tank was the vertical volute spring suspension system (VVSS). The VVSS provided excellent suspension for armored vehicles during road and cross-country movement through a configuration of coiled springs in the shape of cones, or volutes. During operation the coils would slide over one another, compressing to absorb the shock and instability of varied terrain.

Mounted vertically in a compact system that included the bogie and a pair of road wheels, the VVSS outperformed other leaf spring, torsion bar, or coil systems that had been previously in use. The vertical volute system entered service with the US Army in the mid-1930s and was installed on the M1 Combat Car at the Rock Island Arsenal in 1937. The VVSS was also installed in the M2 light tank and the subsequent M3 and M5 series of Stuart light tanks.

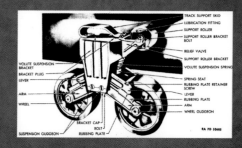

The VVSS was then retained with the development of the M2 medium tank along with the M3 medium tank that entered production in August 1941. From there, due to its availability and satisfactory performance in earlier models, the VVSS was retained in the design and production of the legendary M4 Sherman medium tank.

During extended deployments and combat operations, the VVSS was found to have a relatively short useful life, particularly with the increasing weight of tanks and their heavy weapons as World War II progressed. When the M4A3 Sherman variant was introduced in late 1942, the vertical volute suspension was gradually replaced in some of the production tanks with a horizontal volute suspension system (HVSS). Those M4A3s equipped with the HVSS were designated M4A3E8 and nicknamed "Easy Eight" because of the tank's relatively smooth ride.

The HVSS was heavier and stronger than its predecessor, permitted the changing of individual wheels if necessary, and extended the useful life of the tank's wheels as well. The horizontal configuration utilized a volute spring that was compressed either by the front- or rear-wheel arm of the bogie, transferring energy to the opposing arm and maintaining pressure on the tank's track and the terrain surface.

Above: A page from an M4 maintenance manual calls out the various components of the suspension system. *Voyageur Press collection*

Left: Shown during field-testing in 1942, this close-up view shows a volute spring suspension assembly as well as the large drive sprocket, responsible for supplying power to the tracks of the armored vehicle. The suspension spring is behind the vertical plate atop the peak formed by the two suspension arms. This trial run took place on the grounds of a manufacturing facility in the eastern United States. *William M. Rittase/ US Office of War Information/Library of Congress*

Halted at a refueling post at Fort Knox, Kentucky, an M4 Sherman tank (left) and an M3 Grant/Lee tank (right) display their similarities and their striking differences in design. The M3 entered production as a stopgap measure to combat German tanks with heavier guns. Its main weapon was a hull-mounted 75mm gun, while a 37mm cannon was placed in a small rotating turret. *Alfred T. Palmer/US Office of War Information/Library of Congress*

Early M4 tanks are put through their paces during extensive evaluation in 1942. The M4 was developed with a sense of urgency as Allied armor was improved to cope with the superior German tanks that appeared on the battlefield during World War II in North Africa. The M4 combined the best qualities of its predecessor, the M3 Lee/Grant tank, with several notable improvements. *Voyageur Press collection*

The basic conception, design, field testing, and sustained production of the M4 Sherman were accomplished in a matter of months. Just weeks after the final specifications for the M3 medium tank were approved, the varied options for its successor were put forward at the army's Rock Island Arsenal, located on a small island in the Mississippi River between the cities of Davenport, Iowa, and Rock Island, Illinois.

The most expedient path to the new tank was the one chosen. Again, it involved the incorporation of as many elements of the obsolescent M2 and M3 as possible while providing a medium tank that could

take on German armor, if necessary, with a reasonable prospect of winning. At best, on the face of it the premise seemed contradictory.

The new tank had to provide substantial firepower. It had to be reliable and require relatively low maintenance in the field, and it had to be of such simple design that it could be produced on a massive scale. During their early discussions, military planners were acutely aware that the industrial capacity of any nation, even one that was so rich in manpower and resources as the United States, would be sorely tested with the production of enough tanks that were at

least adequate in performance to equip the armies of much of the Free World in the fight against the Axis. Obviously, multiple defense contractors would be engaged in the production of the new tank at the same time.

Once again, the hull of the M3 and the vertical volute spring suspension served as the basic platform for a new armored vehicle. The experimentation that had taken place both in light and medium tanks during the 1930s paid huge dividends as the preliminary assessment of the new tank's necessary attributes came into focus. Additional components that were derived and validated in earlier tanks and eventually found their way into the T6 and the production M4 designs included the proven rear-mounted Wright Continental R975 EC2 radial engine, tracks with rubber bushings that provided better road and cross country performance than other contemporary tanks, and the same five-speed manual transmission with a single reverse gear. The M4 also introduced the cast hull manufacturing process to medium tank production.

Perhaps some of the stiffest competition for the T6 during its research and early production phases came from the prototype T7, which had been designed originally as a replacement for the M3 and M5 light tanks. Built at the Rock Island Arsenal in January 1942, the first experimental T7 offered the advantage of a much lower silhouette than the M3 medium tank. It provided good visibility for its driver and commander and initially mounted a 37mm gun in a small turret. The original T7 continued in the light tank classification even with additional protective armor, a heavier broad turret, and a more powerful 57mm gun. Its weight soared from thirteen tons to twenty-five tons and taxed the performance of its Wright R975 engine.

In late 1942, while the M4 was in production, senior commanders of the army's Armored Force requested a T7 that would mount a 75mm gun—probably in direct response to the news that the Germans had begun deploying high-velocity 75mm cannon on the PzKpfw. IV during the latter stages of the war in North Africa. The resulting T7E2 accommodated the 75mm main gun in a reinforced turret. Armor protection ranged from three-quarters of an inch on upper surfaces of the hull to two and one-half inches across the front and above the tracks. The tank weighed twenty-eight tons.

Like the M4, the turret of the T7 traversed 360 degrees, and a gyrostabilizer augmented the accuracy of the 75mm gun. However, the tank was substantially overweight, and its engine could not provide the needed horsepower for effective and efficient operation. In the midst of the ramp-up of M4 Sherman production, International Harvester won a contract for the manufacture of three thousand T7 medium tanks. However, the contract was abruptly canceled after only seven of these were completed. At the eleventh hour, it was realized that the T7 could not measure up to the combination of speed and firepower that were exhibited in the M4.

In developing the design of the M4, American engineers began with the basic premise that the flaws in the M3 had to be corrected. In addition, speed, firepower, and armor protection—the three pillars that constituted a successful tank blueprint—had to be balanced to the extent possible. Although armor meant protection for the crew and its relative thickness provided greater survivability in combat in the event that the tank was hit by an enemy shell, it also meant greater weight, which in turn increased cost and demanded larger quantities of precious steel while reducing the tank's speed and complicating the manufacturing process. Further, thousands of tanks were needed in North Africa and later in Europe, and every one of them would reach the battlefield only after a voyage of several thousand miles in the hold of a cargo ship. The greater the weight of the individual tank, the fewer armored vehicles and other critical war materiel could be transported in a given time interval.

The positive and negative aspects of the new design were weighed, and eventually it was decided to sacrifice armor protection in the name of speed and the potential ease of mass production. Although the decision eventually became the source of a controversy that has raged for the last seventy-five years as historians, veterans, and other observers have evaluated the combat performance of the Sherman during World War II, it must be remembered that the idea was in keeping with the prevailing armored doctrine of the United States Army at the time.

When the Chrysler Corporation initiated the production of armored vehicles at the Detroit Tank Arsenal, the facility initially produced the M3 Grant/Lee tank as shown at left. This image depicts the transition to the M4 Sherman, shown on the assembly line at right. *William Vandivert/The LIFE Picture Collection/Getty Images*

Its main weapon secured in a forward position, this completed M4 Sherman medium tank awaits final outfitting for deployment overseas. This upgunned Sherman, with its 76mm cannon meant to provide better antitank performance, was not available until 1944. *US Army*

The M4 was intended as a breakthrough and exploitation weapon—not as a platform for tank versus tank combat. The short-barreled 75mm M2 cannon that initially armed the M4 was deemed adequate in the event that the Sherman met the German PzKpfw. III and PzKpfw. IV tanks that were commonly deployed on the battlefields in late 1941 and early 1942.

Perhaps more properly, the postwar criticism of the Sherman performance should reside with the slow development of a heavy tank to take on the upgunned PzKpfw. IV, PzKpfw. V Panther, and PzKpfw. VI Tiger tanks deployed by the Germans later in World War II. The heavy M26 Pershing tank

saw only limited deployment during the last days of the war in Europe, while the Tank Destroyer Doctrine dictated that the destruction of enemy tanks was to be accomplished with the fast, open-turreted, and heavily armed tank destroyers that first appeared in combat during the final stages of the North African Campaign in late 1943.

The M4's rapid development culminated shortly after the prototype was completed at Aberdeen Proving Ground, and the iconic medium tank entered production in February 1942. Although its upper hull was substantially reconfigured, the resemblance of the M4 to its immediate predecessor was readily apparent.

The tank's external propulsion system included a front drive sprocket connected to the gearbox, a rear-adjustable track idler, three sets of bogies each with a pair of large road wheels with rubber coverings, and three return rollers. The track included seventy-eight links, a configuration that had been standard since the introduction of the M1 Combat Car in 1937. These links were reinforced in the M4 and decreased the tank's ground pressure to improve mobility.

Although there were periodic variations in the M4's powerplant, equipment, and design characteristics, the basic specifications of the original medium tank and the seven main production variants that followed were generally quite similar. The primary M4 medium tank included a turret that was cast in a single piece of steel and incorporated a basket that turned the fighting compartment with the turret via an electrically powered rotation system. The radio, intercom system, and a pair of portable fire extinguishers were contained in the turret along with a ready supply of 75mm ammunition.

Above: This rear view of a DD (Duplex Drive) Sherman tank provides a glimpse of the apparatus that allowed the tank to maneuver in reasonably shallow and calm water to reach a nearby beach. The DD Sherman was developed for operations on D-Day and achieved mixed results as many were swamped in the churning English Channel and failed to reach the shoreline while others came ashore and provided much needed fire support to Allied infantry. *Voyageur Press collection*

Left: This 1945 photo depicts the same Duplex Drive Sherman with its canvas curtain deployed to hold back the surrounding water as it plunges into a lake during field tests. Once the vehicle reached the beach, its canvas curtain would be collapsed, allowing the tank to operate normally. *Voyageur Press collection*

Opposite: After a day of training together, M3 tanks are parked in bivouac at Fort Knox, Kentucky. The M3 and M4 shared many common components, which sped the manufacturing process and introduction of the M4 to the battlefield in Europe and the Pacific during World War II. *Alfred T. Palmer/US Office of War Information/Library of Congress*

131189

The upper hull was initially welded, although it was later cast and rounded in the M4A1. Its glacis was sloped sixty-three degrees and increased the protective properties of the steel, and its flat sides were generally considered conspicuous, adding to the readily identifiable silhouette of the M4 on the battlefield. The lower hull was most often welded, and the bogies were bolted on to facilitate field maintenance. Although a cast hull was preferred from a ballistics standpoint, the process required a large casting and lengthened manufacturing time.

As World War II progressed, improvements in the welding process resulted in properties that approached and then surpassed the ballistics of a cast hull. Flat plates of rolled homogeneous armor (RHA) were welded together, and the rolling process actually strengthened the steel. Initial armor thickness ranged from 2.99 inches on the glacis and frontal area to 1.96 inches on the turret and upper sides and 1.18 inches in less vulnerable areas. Four hatches were available for ingress and egress—two on the hull above the front glacis, one atop the turret, and another on the floor behind the driver's seat.

Three crewmen, including the commander at the rear, the gunner forward on the right, and the loader forward and to the left of the gun breech, were stationed within the turret itself. Their seats were adjustable an entire foot either up or down and five inches forward or backward. The gunner acquired targets for the main 75mm weapon through a telescopic sight that was synchronized with the main gun and used a hand wheel to aim the big gun. Firing on the move was made more accurate with a hydraulic gyrostabilization system, and the weapon was discharged with a foot-operated switch. A .30-caliber Browning M1919A4 machine gun was also mounted in the gun mantlet, while a .50-caliber Browning M2HB machine gun was mounted on the turret hatch for defense against enemy infantry or aircraft.

The driver was positioned in the front of the hull and to the left, while his assistant sat to the right with access to a ball-mounted .30-caliber Browning M1919A4 machine gun. The operation of this machine gun was the assistant driver's primary responsibility. The driver manipulated the Spicer gearbox with levers, and the four-hundred-horsepower R975 engine was capable of moving the thirty-three-ton M4 at a top speed of twenty-nine miles per hour. The M4 engine space contained an auxiliary generator to assist with starting in cold weather and a pair of fire extinguishers that were within reach of a crewman from the fighting compartment or turret area. Twin tanks held 175 gallons of eighty-octane gasoline that provided a range of about 120 miles.

In the field, the Sherman lived up to its expectations in terms of reliability. Some reports indicated that a single tank could operate for an extended period, up to 2,500 miles, with little or no maintenance. This was in sharp contrast to German tanks that were notorious for mechanical breakdowns.

Each of the five crewmen was provided with an excellent field of vision through periscopes. Early M4s included vision slits for the driver and assistant driver. These were protected by bulletproof glass and hinged covers but were eliminated on later models.

The bulk of the M4's heavy ammunition was stored in forward hull compartments. Early models used dry storage; however, combat experience dictated that wet storage would minimize the likelihood of a catastrophic explosion of the 75mm

rounds when the tank was hit. The .30-caliber machine guns were provided with 4,750 rounds of ammunition, while the .50-caliber was armed with three hundred rounds.

As the production of the M4 began, the nature of combat in World War II continued to evolve and would later define the iconic tank's place in history. During the course of the war, the role of infantry support fell increasingly to the Sherman, as did the likelihood of tank versus tank encounters with German armored vehicles. Nevertheless, when employed in the context of its original conception, that of a fast-moving, low-maintenance armored spearhead that packed a substantial punch, the M4 Sherman proved itself in the crucible of war as being well suited to the task.

In the heat of combat on the island of Bougainville in the Pacific, soldiers of the US Army's 37th Infantry Division use an M4 Sherman tank nicknamed "Lucky Legs II" for cover as they fire at Japanese positions in the deep jungle. The M4 Sherman offered mobile firepower that was highly effective against Japanese emplacements in the Pacific during World War II. *Library of Congress*

Above: This 1944 Hercules Cellulose advertisement depicts an M4 Sherman tank utilizing a brightly colored recognition panel to identify the armored vehicle as friendly to Allied aircraft hunting enemy targets from above. The company also notes numerous other wartime uses for its plastics. *Voyageur Press collection*

Right: During maneuvers in the California desert in 1944, a machine gunner aboard an M4 Sherman tank aims his .50-caliber Browning M2 machine gun skyward. The M4 was also equipped with .30-caliber machine guns for use against enemy infantry. *PhotoQuest/Getty Images*

CHAPTER FOUR

Mass Production

Never before or since has the industrial capacity of the United States been as sorely tested as during the years immediately preceding World War II through its conclusion. The challenges of war production were colossal, particularly considering the demands of both domestic and Allied military establishments, varied specifications, and the simple fact that the US economy and manufacturing base had not been on a war footing in a generation.

The American automobile industry was destined to play a major role in the manufacture of vehicles of every type required by the military, and the most prominent of these was the armored fighting vehicle—particularly the modern tank. Despite their robust production capacity, on the eve of World War II

American auto manufacturers were still reeling from the Great Depression and completed only 2.5 million units in 1938. When President Franklin D. Roosevelt called upon the US industrial base to become the great "Arsenal of Democracy" in a radio broadcast on December 29, 1940, few skilled workers in America had even seen a tank.

President Roosevelt recognized that the national security of the United States, facing the threat of the Axis powers—Germany, Italy, and Japan—in Europe and the Pacific, depended on keeping Great Britain in the fight against Hitler and Nazi Germany. Even prior to the British declaration of war on Germany on September 3, 1939, the Roosevelt administration had sanctioned the shipment of raw materials and equipment to Britain in

US industrial capacity provided the Allied war effort in World War II with thousands of tanks, planes, and small arms. The M4 Sherman tank was mass produced at numerous facilities in the United States. Here, a line of M4s nears completion at an assembly plant in Cleveland, Ohio, on April 15, 1942. The tanks are ready for turrets and guns to be mounted at a manufacturing facility in the city's Ordnance District. *Popperfoto/Getty Images*

anticipation of hostilities. When the US Congress passed the Lend-Lease Act in March 1941, the president was authorized to supply war materiel to "the government of any country whose defense the President deems vital to the defense of the United States."

At the suggestion of financier and businessman Bernard Baruch, Roosevelt approached William S. Knudsen, president of General Motors, asking him to accept a commission in the US Army as a lieutenant general and take on awesome responsibilities as the chairman of the Office of Production Management and a member of the National Defense Advisory Commission. Born in Copenhagen, Denmark, in 1879, Knudsen had immigrated to the United States in 1900. He had worked for the Ford Motor Company during the era in which methods of mass production were being refined.

By 1924, Knudsen has risen to the presidency of the Chevrolet Division of General Motors, a position he held for the next thirteen years. In 1937, he was

appointed president of GM, and despite the economic uncertainty of the Depression years the giant automotive manufacturer had remained viable. He accepted President Roosevelt's overture along with an annual salary of one dollar. When his army commission was formally approved in January 1942, it was the highest US military rank ever conferred directly upon a civilian.

Highly experienced and influential, Knudsen helped to leverage American industrial output before and during World War II to extraordinary levels. When victory was achieved, he told the media, "We won because we smothered the enemy in an avalanche of production, the like of which he had never seen, nor dreamed possible."

Although various sources offer slightly differing production numbers, from September 1941 through July 1945, an estimated total of 49,234 M4 Sherman tanks in seven primary variants were manufactured. By far the largest single producer of the M4 was the

Stacked in a converted heater factory in the Midwest, bogey wheels are ready for assembly to complete M4 Sherman tanks. American industry converted rapidly from peacetime manufacturing to a wartime footing and produced staggering amounts of war materiel. This photo was taken in 1942. *Alfred T. Palmer/US Office of War Information/ Library of Congress*

On the floor of a converted heater factory in the Midwestern United States, finished bogey wheel springs await assembly in the suspensions of M4 Sherman tanks. These springs were integral components of a suspension system that provided excellent cross-country mobility for the M4 Sherman. *Alfred T. Palmer/US Office of War Information/ Library of Congress*

Chrysler Corporation with a tally that approached eighteen thousand. The story of Chrysler's substantial commitment to the production of the M4 is remarkable in itself. In a real sense, peacetime rivals became wartime partners.

On June 7, 1940, only a week after President Roosevelt's initial overture to Knudsen, the General Motors executive was on the telephone from his office in Washington, DC. At the other end of the line was Kaufman Thuma Keller, the president of Chrysler. Knudsen explained that he would soon be coming to Detroit, Michigan, the center of the US automotive industry, and that he wanted to meet with Keller. The following Sunday the two men sat down together in Grosse Ile in suburban Detroit.

Getting to the point, Knudsen asked, "How would Chrysler like to build some tanks for the army?" Keller's reply was affirmative. "We certainly would," he said.

Hull components of an M4 Sherman tank are pieced together on the floor of a manufacturing facility in the eastern United States. This photo was taken in 1942 as production of the M4 accelerated and supplanted that of the M3 Grant/Lee tank.
William M. Rittase/US Office of War Information/ Library of Congress

A skilled factory worker performs a function that prepares an M4 Sherman tank's turret for installation. Thousands of workers across the United States produced approximately fifty thousand M4 tanks during World War II, and these, in turn, were provided to the military forces of America's allies as well. *William M. Rittase/US Office of War Information/Library of Congress*

Keller, who was always addressed as either K. T. or Mr. Keller, had previously worked for the Metzger Motor Car Company and the Hudson Motor Company. He joined General Motors in 1911, and then left for a short time before returning to the Buick Division of GM as its general master mechanic.

When Keller came back to Buick, the division president was Walter Chrysler. Sometime later, Chrysler left General Motors to form his own automotive company. He told a colleague, "I wish we had Keller with us and not against us."

Keller came to work for Chrysler in 1926 as vice president of manufacturing and integrated the newly acquired Dodge subsidiary into the corporation. By 1935, Keller had risen to the presidency of Chrysler,

and under his leadership the company's production topped one million units for the first time.

The Chrysler commitment to tank production facilitated the production of the M4 Sherman, and by the end of the World War II more Shermans had been manufactured than any other armored fighting vehicle of the war years with the exception of the fabled Soviet T-34 medium tank. Approximately fifty-five thousand T-34s were built from the late 1930s through 1945.

Events progressed rapidly, although not without significant challenges. The initial Chrysler tank building foray was a tremendous learning experience. Keller met with key Chrysler executives on the Monday morning after his visit with Knudsen and then telephoned Maj. Gen. Charles M. Wesson,

the US Army's chief of ordnance, to ask where the Chrysler men might go to see an actual tank. Wesson sent them to the Rock Island Arsenal, where three prototype models of the M2A1 light tank were being built.

While at Rock Island the Chrysler team asked for blueprints of the M2A1, and these arrived in Detroit two weeks later. Before its assembly lines could build a tank, costs had to be determined, a wooden model had to be completed, and a workable manufacturing process had to be devised. The engineers worked virtually around the clock, spreading plans and spec sheets on the bare floor of the Dodge plant on Conant Street.

The construction of the wooden model was crucial in the learning process. The timbers were shellacked and then fitted together with the tightest tolerances possible. If the shellac was scratched, it meant that changes to the specifications were needed. Along the way, it was determined that the assembly lines that had previously produced automobiles could be adapted with relative ease to build tanks.

One month after their involvement in the project began, the Chrysler engineers delivered the wooden model of the M2A1 without a scratch along with the cost estimate for its production. Machinery had to be prepared, including tooling, and the estimated cost

A machinist fashions bogey wheel brackets in bulk for installation in the suspension system of an M4 Sherman tank. The assembly line production of the M4 was fed by millions of components that were prefabricated to accelerate the pace of the manufacturing process. *William M. Rittase/US Office of War Information/Library of Congress*

A factory worker poses with a completed bogey wheel assembly that will soon be attached to the suspension of an M4 Sherman tank. This photo was taken on the floor of a manufacturing facility in the eastern United States as production of the M4 ramped up in July 1942. *William M. Rittase/US Office of War Information/Library of Congress*

per tank was $33,500. Chrysler projected its production capacity at ten tanks per day, and the army responded that its budget would allow payment for five. A contract for one thousand M2A1s was issued in July, and six weeks later it was abruptly canceled.

The pace of technology, with the belligerents upgunning and increasing the armor of the tanks then fighting in Europe, had outstripped the capabilities of the M2A1, which was declared obsolete. However, within months the M3 and M4 medium tanks would be in production. Eventually, the M4 would be rolling off the assembly lines of ten different defense contractors.

As American production crept toward a war footing, Keller stepped forward as a man of vision. He realized that the number of tanks required by the US Army and the armies of its future allies on the battlefield meant that production had to achieve staggering results, with quantities that would never have been contemplated during peacetime. The fact that American tank design and development had lagged behind that of nearly every other major power on Earth during the previous decade only served to exacerbate the challenge.

Keller contacted General Wesson with a landmark proposal. "Why don't you have a tank arsenal?" he suggested. "With the increasing role of tanks in war, you are going to need a place where you can design, build, test, and repair tanks. A good place for this piece of permanent apparatus would be in Detroit alongside such a pool of labor as we have at Chrysler. Have the arsenal set up and ready to run. When you want tanks, we move in and make tanks for you; when you no longer want tanks, we move back in and, pray God, make automobiles."

Wesson was enthusiastic, saying, "That's exactly what we want—a self-contained, permanent tank arsenal machining even its own armor plate, and maybe the Army can find the money to pay for it."

Keller had made his original proposal with M2A1 production in mind, but even after the cancellation of the first Chrysler tank contract with the Ordnance Department the logic remained sound. The idea was approved, and the US government agreed to foot the bill for the arsenal and lease the facility to Chrysler. In turn, Chrysler would supervise the construction and take responsibility for the necessary equipment. A 113-acre farm site located in Warren Township, seventeen miles from downtown Detroit, was selected for the massive project.

On September 9, 1940, ground was broken for the Detroit Arsenal Tank Plant. While the future remained uncertain concerning US entry into World War II—Pearl Harbor was still more than a year away—there were issues related to the construction of the arsenal. There was no precedent for it; therefore, decisions

involving the size and layout of the physical plant and the number of skilled workers required to operate it were estimated to the best of the ability of the Chrysler and Ordnance Department personnel.

By January 1941, the gigantic arsenal, designed in the Moderne style by renowned industrial architect Albert Kahn, had begun to take shape. Structural steel had been erected while roofing and walls were put in place, making about one-third of the factory ready for use. At the end of the month, the blueprints for the prototype of the M3 medium tank arrived at the arsenal. An unfinished manufacturing facility was expected to produce the prototype of a new tank. Time was short, and the challenge was daunting. Nevertheless, the arsenal and its initial product took shape at the same time.

On April 12, 1941, ten weeks after the arrival of the plans for the M3 at the arsenal, the two prototype M3s, one after the other, rolled out of the arsenal before a gathering of two thousand people, including the governor of Michigan, the mayor of Detroit, Keller, and Generals Wesson and Adna Chaffee Jr., chief of the army's recently created Armored Force. By June, the arsenal was substantially completed, and the first production M3 rolled off the assembly line on July 8. The massive Detroit tank arsenal extended five city blocks long and two blocks wide, while its initial assembly line stretched 1,850 feet. Employees were being hired at the phenomenal rate of two hundred per day, and orders for more tanks poured in from the Ordnance Department.

B.E. Hutchinson, a vice president of Chrysler's Plymouth Division, was tasked with managing the Detroit Arsenal Tank Plant. At the end of July, the arsenal employed approximately 2,200 people. That number more than doubled during the next two weeks, and by late August 1942 more than six thousand people were working on three assembly lines. In time, the number of assembly lines would increase to five. Hutchinson offered a seven-day work week to the Ordnance Department but did not recommend it due to safety concerns that might emerge with employee fatigue. He did institute a six-day work week with around-the-clock shifts.

As production of the M3 ramped up, Keller received word from the Ordnance Department that the specifications for the M4 medium tank were nearing completion. General Levin H. Campbell Jr. informed the Chrysler executive on September 8, 1941, that the Ordnance Department wanted the M4 in production as soon as possible. Chrysler was also asked to build a pair of early-production, or pilot, tanks. Within a week of learning that the pace of M4 production was to be quickened, Keller was informed that the army wanted the company to present a proposal to reach an output of 750 M4s per month as soon as possible.

Although none of its executives, engineers, or production people had even seen drawings of an M4 tank, Chrysler agreed to the ambitious undertaking. The first thing that had to be accomplished was the extension of the existing assembly lines to 2,300 feet, 450 feet longer than the M3 lines. Quickly, the Chrysler management team came to the realization that such a production quota would require a dozen other company plants to be dedicated to producing the new M4. Scores of additional subcontractors would need to be identified and then signed on to produce components. Chrysler had already throttled back its automobile production, and during the first quarter of 1942 all automobile manufacturing was halted in preparation for the coming of the M4.

The Ordnance Departments steadily requested increases in production, and on December 1, 1941, the arsenal's five hundredth tank, an M3, was completed.

Left: Several Sherman tanks advance along an assembly line in various stages of completion in this early photo taken on April 21, 1942. These tanks are the M4A1 variant, the first to enter mass production. The Lima Locomotive Works in Lima, Ohio, turned out the first production M4A1 tanks beginning in February 1942. *Voyageur Press collection*

Opposite: The steel hulls of M4 Sherman tanks sit on the factory floor next to bogey wheel assemblies that will be installed in their chassis. The combination of mass production and reliability made the M4 a war winner despite its shortcomings. *William M. Rittase/US Office of War Information/Library of Congress*

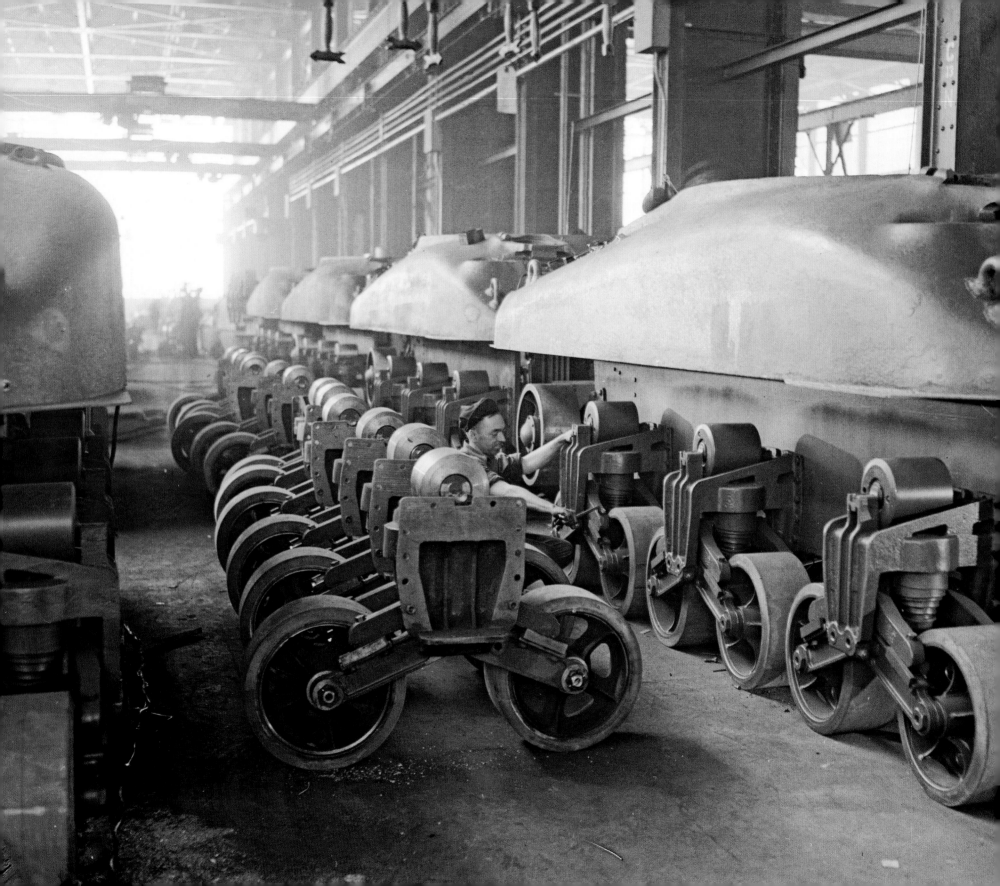

President Roosevelt Tours
the Detroit Tank Arsenal

On September 18, 1942, President Franklin D. Roosevelt visited the Detroit Arsenal Tank Plant during an unpublicized tour of manufacturing facilities that had been converted or constructed to produce war materiel and training camps that were preparing soldiers for deployment overseas.

Detroit was Roosevelt's first tour stop, and the event was kept secret for security reasons. Few people at the arsenal were aware that such a distinguished visitor would be arriving that day, but when the president's special train was seen actually backing into the massive factory where the new M4 medium tank was in production, news of his arrival buzzed throughout the facility.

Accompanied by an entourage that included Mrs. Roosevelt and Donald Nelson, chairman of the War Production Board, the president of the United States met Chrysler Corporation President K. T. Keller, who served as the tour

guide while the party viewed the assembly lines and rode through the arsenal in a car. All the while, the facility was said to have been operating normally. Drivers gunned the engines of forty finished tanks—probably M4s—on the outdoor test track, and workers went about their assigned tasks.

Nelson was impressed and commented, "This is the most amazing production job I have ever seen."

To preserve the tour's tight security, President Roosevelt made no official remarks about his arsenal experience until he returned to Washington, DC, several days later. In a White House press conference, he related with a grin that the arsenal provided "an amazing demonstration of what can be done by the right organization, spirit, and planning."

During a 1965 interview, Keller remembered the extraordinary security measures that were enacted before the president's visit and his discussion with Mike Reilly, head of the Secret Service. "So Reilly came up to see me about three weeks ahead of that, making the arrangements and how they were going to get the president in. And I lay it all out for him," said Keller. "'This is to be very secret,' he [Reilly] said. 'Now, the president wants you to keep the plant running because he wants to see how you build a tank.'

". . . And I said, 'If you want to have it look as though the plant is running, you get me up enough Secret Service men and I will put them on the machines along the line and break them in.' I got a flock of Secret Service fellows and we had them all running on machines. And we laid this tour out through there."

Near the end of the visit, President Roosevelt's car ventured over to the test track where the tanks were rolling. He asked Keller, "Do you allow smoking out here?"

Keller replied, "Please light up. I am dying to have one myself."

More than thirty years after President Roosevelt came to the Detroit Tank Arsenal, Keller recalled that the two men had gotten along quite well—so well in fact that the Chrysler executive was then trusted to "look after" dignitaries from foreign countries who came to Detroit.

Completed M4 Sherman tanks sit on the floor of the Detroit Tank Arsenal awaiting shipment to the US military and final destinations overseas. Chrysler Corporation produced thousands of M4s at the Detroit Arsenal, a vast industrial complex that was conceived, constructed, and became fully operational during World War II. *Voyageur Press collection*

An M4 Sherman tank awaits the installation of tracks on the factory floor in this photo dated September 1942. The installation of tracks was usually the final step in the manufacturing process prior to shipping the tank to a military depot for final preparations. *Popperfoto/Getty Images*

Just three months later, the 1,100th tank was finished and sent to the Soviet Union via Lend-Lease. Production reached more than 360 tanks in March 1942, and in the same month the final specifications for the M4 were approved. Tooling and equipment were hurriedly placed in service, and the first Chrysler-produced M4 rolled off the arsenal assembly line in Warren Township on July 22, 1942. On August 3, the last of 3,352 M3s was completed. The transition from the old to the new design was practically seamless, or so it appeared to outside observers.

From its inception, the Detroit Arsenal Tank Plant had been the darling of the Ordnance Department. The Roosevelt administration pointed with pride to its contribution to national defense and then to the war effort. The media were continually writing stories about its production capabilities.

An article published in the Detroit Times newspaper heralded, "One of the most remarkable achievements of the automotive industry has been in the tank field. It was a product of which they knew nothing. Chrysler took over this job. It is seven months ahead of schedule on its first order [for the M4] and its present capacity was not even considered possible when it was given its first contract. Since then it has changed over to the new all-welded hull (this was only one of many changes) without interrupting output. If ever the ingenuity of the industry met its test it has been on this job."

As the first chapter of the arsenal's history closed with the final M3 and the second began with the factory-fresh M4, flashbulbs popped and snapped while photographers captured pictures of the two tanks side by side. General Campbell, who rose to chief of the Ordnance Department in 1942, was noticeably impressed. On August 10, he stood atop a flatcar before an assemblage of workers and presented the arsenal with the "E Flag" for production excellence.

Opposite: Treads for new M4 Sherman tanks are stacked adjacent to the assembly line at the American Locomotive Company in Schenectady, New York. American Locomotive was one of many manufacturers across the United States that successfully converted from civilian production to the fabrication of vital arms and armaments during World War II. *Howard R. Hollem/US Office of War Information/Library of Congress*

Right: Frank Hughes, a member of the labor management committee at the American Locomotive Company in Schenectady, New York, sprays drive sprockets prior to their installation on new M4 Sherman tanks. This photo was taken at the factory in 1943. *Howard R. Hollem/US Office of War Information/Library of Congress*

Several brand new M4 tanks were lined up on high ground behind the general, who commented, "We have upped the ante on you time and again, and you have met every demand."

Precious raw materials were always in short supply, and the steel that built M4 tanks also went into the construction of warships for the US Navy. Production priorities resulted in a forty percent reduction in tank quotas at the end of 1942. Chrysler produced 5,004 tanks that year, four more than its assigned goal. Its efficient production rate resulted in lower cost per unit, and the company rebated nearly $8 million to the federal government. In 1943, the arsenal's M4 production peaked at 5,111, and in 1944 nearly 3,100 were finished along with approximately 3,600 of the new M26 Pershing heavy tank, and a rebate check just short of $11 million was sent to the government. More M4s were turned out in 1945 until Chrysler production of the tank ceased in June of that year. Thousands of used M4s were also returned to the arsenal and other facilities for refurbishing and repair during the war years.

From 1941 to 1945, Chrysler Corporation produced nine variants of the M4 medium tank, including four models equipped with a 105mm howitzer designed specifically for close infantry support. The arsenal had served as the catalyst for the company's immense output, generating roughly twenty-five percent of the total wartime US tank production of nearly ninety thousand vehicles. As the facility neared the height of its productivity in the spring of 1943, General Campbell wrote to K. T. Keller, "Words, of course, are totally inadequate to describe how we in Ordnance feel about the accomplishments of the Chrysler tank arsenal."

Chrysler continued to operate the arsenal under government ownership until 1982, when its Defense Division was sold to General Dynamics Land Systems. The M1 Abrams main battle tank was produced there from the 1980s until the facility was closed permanently in 1996. A historical marker pays tribute to the immense contribution the Detroit Arsenal Tank Plant and Chrysler Corporation made to victory in World War II and later to national defense.

Along with Chrysler Corporation, ten other manufacturers built the M4 Sherman tank, its seven main variants, and other vehicles based on its highly adaptable chassis during World War II. The names of some of the companies are quite familiar, while others have passed into obscurity. They included the Lima Locomotive Works, Federal Machine & Welder, Pacific Car & Foundry, the Fisher Body Division of General Motors, Pressed Steel Car Company, Pullman Standard, American Locomotive, Ford Motor Company, Baldwin Locomotive Works, and Aberdeen Proving Ground, where a single T6 prototype, forerunner of the M4, was completed.

Based in Lima, Ohio, the Lima Locomotive Works was the first manufacturer to come online to build the M4A1, the original production variant of the Sherman. In February 1942, the company began producing the M4A1, and, of the ten units initially completed, nine were sent to Aberdeen Proving Ground for testing and evaluation. The tenth tank was shipped to Great Britain. Within a few months,

nearly three hundred were on their way to the British Eighth Army in North Africa.

Founded in 1859, the Lima Locomotive Works produced locomotives for railroads across the United States as well as tanks during World War II. A two-hundred-thousand-square-foot building dedicated to the production of tanks was completed adjacent to the existing plant in 1941, and employment reached a peak of 4,200 people shortly thereafter. During wartime, the Lima Locomotive Works completed 1,655 M4A1 medium tanks. After the war, the company struggled to survive. Its last locomotive was completed

A welding crew works on the partly completed hull of a new M4 tank at the American Locomotive Company's Schenectady, New York, plant. *Howard R. Hollem/US Office of War Information/Library of Congress*

Factory worker Ida F. Molitor operates a heavy-duty overhead traveling crane on the floor of the American Locomotive Company in Schenectady, New York. The mother of two teenage children, she went to work in October 1942 at the company manufacturing M4 Sherman tanks and M7 mobile howitzer carriages. *Howard R. Hollem/US Office of War Information/Library of Congress*

in 1951, and after merger attempts, a change of ownership, and years of manufacturing road-building machinery and cranes, the company eventually closed its doors in 1981.

In an effort to duplicate the apparent success of Chrysler's Detroit tank arsenal, Fisher was approached in September 1941 to build and operate a plant designed specifically to produce the M4 medium tank. In January 1942, construction on the 452,000-square-foot Grand Blanc Tank Arsenal, in Grand Blanc, Michigan, began. By the time M4 production began at Grand Blanc in April, the tanks were already being built in other Fisher facilities as well, and when the war

ended in 1945, Fisher had completed 11,258 of the medium tanks and a total of 21,000 tanks of all types.

Fisher also constructed the M10 tank destroyer, based on the M4 chassis, and manufactured thousands of turrets and hulls for the M18 tank destroyer that was assembled by the Buick Division of GM. Its other contributions included transmission and engine components along with subassemblies for the Boeing B-29 Superfortress heavy bomber.

Although Ford was one of America's Big Three automakers during World War II, its production of M4 medium tanks was limited to just 1,690, along with 1,035 M10 tank destroyers. Rather than fully engaging

Opposite: M4 Sherman tanks and M7 mobile howitzer carriages are completed on the production lines of the American Locomotive Company in Schenectady, New York, in 1943. Along this line of vehicles, an M7 is partially visible in the foreground, followed by three M4s. *Howard R. Hollem/US Office of War Information/Library of Congress*

Left: As Sherman production heated up, so did the drive for the raw materials needed to build the tanks. Posters like this admonished Americans to do their part. *Voyageur Press collection*

Below: This magazine advertisement for the Howell Electric Motors Company praises the valor of the American military and the factory workers in production facilities, as well as the company's own contribution to the war effort. Its focus is an M4 Sherman tank progressing along an assembly line as workers make adjustments to the turret and suspension while tracks are being installed. *Voyageur Press collection*

in the manufacture of finished tanks, Ford produced components in great quantities, including more than twenty-seven thousand tank engines that found their way into M4s and other vehicles on the assembly lines of companies that were peacetime rivals. Two Ford assembly plants, located in Richmond, California, and Chester, Pennsylvania, served as tank depots, receiving tanks from other producers, outfitting them with communications gear and weaponry, and preparing them for shipping overseas. The company was a principal builder of the iconic Jeep during the war.

Ford's most famous and controversial wartime production facility was the massive 3.5-million-square-foot Willow Run plant near Ypsilanti, Michigan, built to manufacture the Consolidated B-24 Liberator bomber. At its peak, Willow Run employed approximately forty-two thousand workers. Approximately one-third of them were women.

In 1899, the Pressed Steel Car Company incorporated in New Jersey, encompassing the operations of several concerns that were engaged in the production of railway cars and components for automobiles and trucks. During World War II, its manufacturing facility in Hegewisch on the southeast side of Chicago built both the M3 and M4 medium tanks. By 1945, a total of 8,147 M4s had been

Arthur Hale, a toolmaker with the American Locomotive Company in Schenectady, New York, for forty years, operates a milling machine during the production of M4 Sherman tanks in 1943. Hale was responsible for developing a process that saved time and steel, a valuable contribution to the war effort. *Howard R. Hollem/US Office of War Information/Library of Congress*

completed there. The facility employed large numbers of women, who augmented the wartime workforce, and in September 1942 several of these female workers posed for photographers with an M4 after attending an awards ceremony at the plant.

The Pullman Standard Car Company was a descendant of the original Pullman Palace Car Company incorporated by George Pullman in 1867 to build railway cars. Companies engaged in the railroad industry during peacetime delivered approximately twenty percent of US tank production during World War II. The Pullman manufacturing facility in Hammond, Indiana, was one of many that built the M4, and a total of 3,426 were finished in Pullman factories by war's end.

The American Locomotive Company of Schenectady, New York, produced 2,300 M4 medium tanks during World War II along with tank destroyers, shells, bombs, and gun mounts. The company also built diesel engines and turbochargers at its facility in Auburn, New York, and its employment tripled to fifteen thousand people from 1941 to 1945. The company continued its primary business, the manufacture of locomotives, finishing nearly 4,500 during the war years. The company was founded in 1901 with the combining of seven competing entities, and subsidiaries worked in the automobile industry and the nuclear energy field before it closed permanently in 1969.

Founded in 1830, the venerable Baldwin Locomotive Works of Eddystone, Pennsylvania, produced both M3 and M4 tanks, including 1,245 of the latter, along with locomotives and switchers during World War II. The company went out of business in 1972. Pacific Car & Foundry of Bellevue, Washington, built 926 M4s, and today the company is a member of the Fortune 500, ranking third in the world in the manufacture of medium and heavy trucks. The small Federal Machine & Welder Company completed 540 M4s.

By the spring of 1944, only three of the original M4 manufacturers—Chrysler, Fisher, and the Pressed Steel Car Company—were still producing the tanks due to

greater emphasis on the heavier M26 Pershing tank and reductions in quotas because of rising demands for steel in the shipbuilding industry.

The Montreal Locomotive Works of Canada produced the Ram I and II tanks and numerous variants from the autumn of 1941 through 1943. The Ram utilized the modified chassis of the M3 medium tank and, therefore, shared several design characteristics with the M4. However, it was used for training purposes in Canada and Britain and was never deployed to combat areas. During a limited production run from September to December 1943, Montreal Locomotive Works completed 188 Grizzly I tanks, modified versions of the American M4A1.

During the course of World War II, US allies received thousands of M4 medium tanks through Lend-Lease. Great Britain alone was the recipient of more than seventeen thousand, while the Soviet Union took more than four thousand and Free French forces received nearly seven hundred.

PART III

The SHERMAN GOES TO WAR

CHAPTER FIVE

Variants and Innovations

The M4 Sherman tank in all its variations proved both in war and later in peace that it rates among history's most versatile armored vehicles. The Sherman's service life lasted well beyond half a century, and some examples may in fact remain in service today.

Considering that the design, production, and deployment of the Medium Tank M4 constitute the epitome of a "rush job" spurred by the exigencies of war, such longevity is nothing short of astounding. The development of the M2 light tank and the M3 medium tank contributed greatly to the swiftness with which the M4 became available. However, even more remarkable is the fact that key components of the M4 were introduced and modified in the midst of wartime production.

During the interwar years, the US military had devoted precious little in the way of tangible resources, financial or otherwise, to the development of tanks. On the eve of World War II, existing components were hurriedly combined in the series of vehicles leading up to the introduction of the M4. The use of the vertical volute suspension system and the modified hull of the earlier M3 are indicative of this urgency. So was the immediate lack of a dedicated tank engine. Virtually no prewar funding had been appropriated for the development of an engine specifically designed to power a modern armored fighting vehicle. The immediate solution in 1940 was the modification of the nine-cylinder Continental R-975 radial aircraft engine for use in American-built tanks.

An M4 Sherman tank (foreground) throws up a cloud of dust during maneuvers in 1942. Although there were similarities in design and component parts, the M4 was a considerable improvement over its predecessor, the M3 (background). *Alfred T. Palmer/US Office of War Information/Library of Congress*

The M4's 1941 to 1945 manufacturing run included seven primary production variants—the M4, M4A1, M4A2, M4A3, M4A4, M4A5, and M4A6—as well as numerous purpose-built or adapted vehicles for infantry support, recovery, antiaircraft defense, limited amphibious capability, mine clearing, and other functions. The progression of models does not indicate successive performance improvement in each type. Rather, a more appropriate description of these types is as concurrent production models incorporating varied components, including different engines, armament, or subtle alterations to the basic tank design, such as hatch size and welded fasteners or handles. Each M4 tank variant weighed approximately thirty tons, and the powerplants produced top speeds of roughly thirty miles per hour.

Early M4s with the short-barreled 75mm M3 L/40 gun were completed with the small D50878 turret. Later variants were upgunned to the high-velocity 76mm M1 L/55 gun, with the larger T23 turret developed to accommodate the heavier weapon.

The M4 variant featured the Continental R-975 radial engine, the short-barreled 75mm M3 L/40 main gun, and a welded hull. It was produced from July 1942 through January 1944 by Chrysler Corporation, Pullman Standard, Baldwin Locomotive Works, American Locomotive Company, and the Pressed Steel Car Company, which combined to complete 6,748 tanks. Chrysler also built the M4(105) and the M4(105) HVSS (horizontal volute spring suspension). Both were equipped with the 105mm M4 howitzer for close infantry support; the latter

Above: Tankers in training fuel a new M4 Sherman tank during maneuvers at Fort Knox, Kentucky, in early 1942. The original caption of this photo calls Fort Knox a place where "men of the armored forces are developed into hard-bitten tankers." *Alfred T. Palmer/US Office of War Information/ Library of Congress*

Opposite: The commander of an M4 Sherman tank uses a signal flag to communicate with other tanks in his formation. This photo was taken while the unit was on maneuvers and probably before the installation of radio equipment, which made coordination between armored vehicles much more practical. *Alfred T. Palmer/US Office of War Information/Library of Congress*

Allied Ammunition

The 75mm, 76mm, and 17-pounder main weapons that were prevalent on Allied tanks and tank destroyers of the World War II era fired a variety of ammunition depending on the combat situation.

The 75mm M3 L/40 gun was intended for an infantry fire support role and to engage both fixed strongpoints and troop concentrations. Engaging enemy tanks was considered the responsibility of contemporary tank destroyer formations; therefore, armor-piercing ammunition was of lower priority, and the array of ammunition carried aboard the M4 Sherman tank reflected that doctrine.

The M48 high-explosive round was used against buildings, lightly fortified positions, and vehicles that were unarmored. It weighed nearly fifteen pounds with 1.5 pounds of explosive TNT providing the power on detonation. The round traveled at a rate of 2,050 feet per second when fired from the standard M3 75mm gun. The fuse could be set at super quick

(SQ) for faster detonation or point detonation (PD) to allow for greater penetration of the target.

The T30 canister round was highly effective against exposed enemy troop concentrations. Used primarily in the Pacific, it consisted of a large casing filled with lethal steel balls that dispersed in all directions on impact. The effect was similar to that of a large shotgun. A smoke round was also available if needed.

The initial armor-piercing round of the M3 was the M72 AP-T (armor-piercing tracer). Its poor performance led to early replacement with the M61A1 APC (armor-piercing capped) shell, which shared some characteristics of a high-explosive round as well. The cap, made of softer metal than the surrounding projectile, functioned to hold the round together, allowing penetration of the target prior to detonation. Theoretically, once penetration was achieved, a small explosive charge at the base of the round would detonate and create extensive damage inside the enemy vehicle.

The muzzle velocity of the M61 round was just over 2,024 feet per second and judged capable of penetrating 3.3 inches of armor at a distance of five hundred yards. However, as the armor protection of second-generation German tanks increased, the performance of the M61 round declined dramatically. These rounds often failed to penetrate sloped frontal armor that was more than three inches thick at reasonable distance, while the 75mm and 88mm guns of the improved German PzKpfw. IV, PzKpfw. V Panther, and PzKpfw. VI Tiger tanks could engage and destroy the Sherman at standoff distances.

Concerns related to the performance of the 75mm M3 gun and the M61 armor-piercing round prompted the upgunning of production Sherman tanks with the 76mm gun M1. This weapon offered better antitank performance as it became obvious that flawed armored doctrine was contributing to an alarming loss rate of Sherman tanks on the Western Front in 1944.

The high-velocity 76mm gun was somewhat inferior to the 75mm in the performance of its high-explosive and smoke rounds; however, its increased firepower with the M62 armor-piercing round provided a substantial improvement in tank versus tank encounters. With a muzzle velocity of 2,600 feet per second, the M62 round was capable of penetrating more than four inches of armor at a distance of 1,100 yards. Other rounds in the 76mm family, including the M79 armor-piercing shell, HVAP (high-velocity armor piercing), and HVAP M93, were capable of even greater penetrations.

Live-fire tests with the Sherman mounting the 76mm gun revealed problems with platform stability and balance. To correct the problem, the tank's turret was modified, and a counterweight was added while the barrel of the weapon was shortened by fifteen inches.

The British QF 17-pounder was used both as a towed antitank weapon and to upgrade the Sherman with a gun believed capable of destroying heavier, late-war German tanks. The 17-pounder fired two types of antitank ammunition. Its armor-piercing capped ballistic capped (APCBC) round could penetrate more than five inches of sloped armor at a distance of nearly 550 yards. At nearly 1,100 yards, it was capable of penetrating more than 4.5 inches of armor.

The 17-pounder also fired an armor-piercing discarding sabot (APDS) round, which utilized a lightweight metal casing or sabot to increase muzzle velocity and stabilization of the round before falling away in flight. The APDS round was live-fire tested to penetrate more than eight inches of sloped armor at a distance of approximately 550 yards and more than 7.25 inches at roughly 1,100 yards.

Opposite: Preparing an M4 Sherman tank for shipment to the battlefield in Europe, a worker at the Chester Tank Depot in Chester, Pennsylvania, applies a packing of grease to the tank's main 75mm gun to protect it from the elements en route to its destination. The 75mm M3 L/40 gun was intended for an infantry fire support role and to engage both fixed strongpoints and troop concentrations. *Voyageur Press collection*

incorporated HVSS. A total of 800 of the M4(105) and 841 of the M4(105) HVSS were finished from February 1944 to March 1945.

The initial production model of the Medium Tank M4 was actually the M4A1, which rolled off the assembly line for the first time at the Lima Locomotive Works in Lima, Ohio, in February 1942. The M4A1 was also powered by the Continental R-975 radial engine and armed with the 75mm M3 L/40 gun. Its hull was cast in a single piece and rounded. A total of 6,281 were completed at the Lima Locomotive Works, Pressed Steel Car Company, and Pacific Car & Foundry by December 1943.

In January 1944, Pressed Steel Car began production of an improved M4A1, the M4A1(76)W, which was upgraded with the high-velocity 76mm M1 main weapon, an improved commander's cupola that included six viewing blocks of three-inch bulletproof glass, and the improved Continental R-975 C1 radial engine. Another significant wartime improvement

The crew of a US Army M4 Sherman tank rests during training exercises at Fort Knox, Kentucky. During World War II, the M4 Sherman became the backbone of the Allied armored forces in the European and Pacific Theaters. Approximately fifty thousand were manufactured from 1942 through 1945.
Alfred T. Palmer/US Office of War Information/ Library of Congress

In this training photo taken at Fort Knox, Kentucky, in 1942, an M4 Sherman tank negotiates a steep incline. The M4 proved extremely versatile in combat, capable of negotiating difficult terrain while its diesel and gasoline powerplants were reliable. *Alfred T. Palmer/US Office of War Information/ Library of Congress*

with the M4A1(76)W was the so-called "wet" storage for ammunition aboard the tank. Combat experience indicated that the dry storage of tank rounds contributed to the incidence of catastrophic explosions if the tank was hit. Wet storage was intended to suppress the combustion of the M4A1 ammunition supply. Fuel tanks were also given the protection of water jackets.

A total of 3,426 M4A1(76)W tanks were produced at Pressed Steel Car through July 1945. The M4A1E8 and M4A1(76)W HVSS subvariants of the M4A1 were equipped with the 76mm M1 gun and the wider suspension.

In April 1942, the M4A2 was introduced, and M4A2(76)W followed in the spring of 1944. The M4A2 was equipped with the General Motors 6046 diesel engine, which was actually a combination of two GM 6-71 diesels. It incorporated the powertrain that was common to the earlier production M3A3 and M3A5 models and was the first M4 variant to be constructed with a welded hull. Its main armament was the 75mm M3 L/40 gun, and additional protection was supplied with appliqué armor on both flanks and at the gunner's position to the left of the turret.

The M4A2 is distinguishable with small hoods above the driver and assistant driver positions along with small hatches. The weight of the tank was increased to approximately thirty-two tons, and its range was curtailed to about one hundred miles.

A brief run of a model designated the M4A2(75) D was built by Fisher and is recognized with larger hatches, while the M4A2E8 included the high-velocity 76mm gun. Produced in the greatest number of any M4 variant, a total of 8,053 M4A2s were built through May 1944 at the factories of Pullman Standard, American Locomotive, Baldwin Locomotive Works, Fisher, and Federal Machine & Welder.

The M4A2(76)W and the HVSS version were manufactured for one year, from May 1944 to May 1945, at Fisher and Pressed Steel Car facilities, and 2,915 were finished. The glacis of the M4A2(76)W was sloped at forty-seven degrees, and its armor protection was 4.25 inches thick, increasing the weight of the tank to more than thirty-three tons. The M4A2E4, equipped with a torsion bar suspension, was evaluated but never put into production.

In June 1942, Ford Motor Company began producing the M4A3 variant powered by the eight-cylinder, liquid-cooled Ford GAA V-8 engine and mounting the 75mm L/40 main weapon. Ford built 1,690 M3A3s, while Chrysler and Fisher completed the balance of 3,071 M4A3s with the 75mm L/40 main gun and wet ammunition storage. These were designated the M4A3(75)W. Earlier M4A3s with dry ammunition storage were often provided with another inch of appliqué armor above the storage bins. This was removed with the introduction of wet storage.

The M4A3 included a cast-steel cover for the transmission case, and the slope of the hull glacis was sixty degrees in the early versions. This was decreased to forty-seven degrees with 4.25-inch thick armor in the late-production M4A3(75)W. Duckbills, longer-end connections for the tracks, were added to some M4A3s

An M4 Sherman medium tank nicknamed "Hurricane" receives a new engine in the field. The M4 gained a reputation as a rugged, reliable tank that was easy to maintain and repair. The engine that is being replaced is hoisted from the tank's hull with an A-frame. Several companies, including General Motors, Chrysler, Ford, and Continental Motors, manufactured engines for the M4 Sherman series of tanks and armored vehicles. *US Army*

to provide better traction in difficult terrain. The driver's position was equipped with direct vision slots and a protective armored cover.

The M4A3(76)W and M4A3(76) HVSS, equipped with the 76mm M1 gun, entered production in March 1944 at Chrysler's Detroit tank arsenal and Fisher facilities. A total of 1,925 M4A3(76)W tanks and 2,617 M4A3(76) HVSS models were built before production ceased in April 1945.

As Allied troops streamed ashore on D-Day, June 6, 1944, a relative handful of M4A3s were modified with the intent that they would better fill the role of impact weapons capable of breaching enemy lines. Just over 250 tanks armed with either the 75mm or 76mm gun were provided with 3.5 inches of appliqué armor that increased glacis protection to a whopping seven inches, effectively doubling the original armored thickness. This version of the M4A3 was later nicknamed the "Jumbo." The weight of the tank soared to more than thirty-eight tons, and the Jumbo was substantially less maneuverable while consuming considerably more fuel than the standard M4A3. However, the variant proved successful in combat, its frontal armor withstanding the best of the German antitank rounds, including the 88mm shells from Tiger tanks and the shaped charges from shoulder-fired weapons such as the Panzerfaust.

One of the best-known M4 variants was the M4A3E8, better known as the "Easy Eight." The Easy Eight also achieved the longest documented period of service, lasting until the 1980s. Powered by the Ford GAA V-8 engine, the Easy Eight earned its nickname due to the smooth ride the HVSS suspension offered with its twenty-three-inch-wide tracks. It also included wet ammunition storage, seven inches of armor protection for the glacis, increased armor protection on each flank, and the large T23 turret mounting the powerful high-velocity 76mm gun. Nearly seventy percent of the M4A3(76)W tanks produced by Fisher and the Detroit Tank Arsenal were classified more succinctly as Easy Eights, and the M4A3E8 was most likely the last M4 tank variant in production.

The M4A3 chassis also mounted the 105mm howitzer in the M4A3(105) and M4A3(105) HVSS self-propelled infantry support vehicles. A total of 3,039 of these weapons were constructed at the Detroit Tank Arsenal.

From July 1942 through November 1943, the Detroit Tank Arsenal completed 7,499 M4A4 tanks. These were powered by the Chrysler multibank engine, which was actually the combination of five standard six-cylinder automobile engines attached to a common crankshaft. The multibank engine was an ingenious response to a critical shortage of tank engines, particularly when the demand for aircraft engines such as the Continental R-975 to be used for their original purpose began to take precedence over tank production. The size of the multibank engine did require a longer hull, and the M4A4 was lengthened nearly six inches to accommodate it.

The American designation M4A5 was reserved for any M4s produced in Canada. Although the M4 was the principal tank of the Canadian Army in World War II, only the Grizzly, substantially a copy of the M4A1, was produced at the Montreal Locomotive Works in late 1943. The company also manufactured the Ram I and II tanks, based on the M3 chassis and therefore similar in design to the M4. There were no tanks formally designated M4A5; however, the Canadians utilized large numbers of the M4A2 and M4A4 after the tank was formally adopted by the Canadian armed forces in the spring of 1943. The Canadians also manufactured the Sexton self-propelled artillery piece, mounting the QF 25-pounder gun atop the Grizzly chassis.

The M4A6, powered by the Caterpillar D200A diesel radial engine, started down the assembly lines at the Detroit Tank Arsenal in October 1943. Only seventy-five examples were completed before production ceased in February 1944, and while some sources state that all of these were utilized as training vehicles in the United States, others assert that some were deployed to the Pacific with US Marine units during World War II.

In addition to those armored fighting vehicles that were identified with the M4 nomenclature, numerous other combat systems were based on the M4 and delivered conspicuous service during World War II and beyond. One of the most famous of these was the 105mm Howitzer Motor Carriage M7 and later the M7B1. Originally designed atop the M3 chassis, the M7 and M7B1 denote the transition to the M4 chassis. This self-propelled artillery piece was given the nickname "Priest" by the British, who used it extensively, in

The cloud of dust churned up in this vivid image of an M4 Sherman tank on maneuvers in June 1942 conveys some sense of the raw power generated by the tank's engines, which were capable of moving it forward at a top speed of more than thirty miles per hour. *Camerique/ Getty Images*

reference to its distinctive round, pulpit-like machine gun ring.

The M7 was based on the chassis of the early M4, and 3,490 were built during the course of World War II. The M7B1 was constructed on the chassis of the M4A3, and 826 were completed from 1944 to the end of the war.

Based on the M4A2 chassis, the M10 Wolverine tank destroyer was officially known as the Gun Motor Carriage M10 and entered production in late 1942. The follow-on M10A1 was constructed atop the M4A3 chassis. Both mounted the high-velocity 76mm gun in an open turret. The M36 Jackson carried a 90mm gun and was also based on the M4A2 and M4A3 chassis.

More than 6,700 of these tank destroyer types were completed from 1942 to 1945.

Nicknamed "Zippo," after a popular cigarette lighter of the day, the M4A3R3 variant mounted a devastating flamethrower and was developed for US Marines in the Pacific late in World War II. It was particularly effective against Japanese strongpoints during the battles of Iwo Jima and Okinawa in early 1945. The M4 Crocodile was an attempt to develop a flamethrower tank for American forces in Western Europe. Following the success of the British Churchill Crocodile, this cooperative effort was undertaken in early 1944 with the British supplying

**MORE POWER FOR TANKS TODAY—
CHEAPER POWER FOR AMERICA TOMORROW!**

America's tanks pack a powerful push as well as a powerful punch. And more times than most people know, this push comes from a General Motors Diesel Engine.

What's more, you'll also find these rugged, hard-working power plants in landing barges, patrol vessels, military trucks, construction tractors and many other wartime jobs where sturdy dependability is required.

They burn cheaper fuel and use less

of it—operate with a minimum of attention.

Of course the needs of war are taking every engine that even our expanded production can make, but when peace comes America will profit—through low-cost power for many new applications.

So while now GM Diesels are adding strength to America's fighting arm, they will be one of the important contributions to better days after victory is ours.

With each war there seems to develop a new era in transportation. And in this one there is the epoch-making General Motors Diesel Locomotive, tried, proved and providing a new pattern of transportation, keyed to the greater days ahead.

GM
GENERAL MOTORS
DIESEL POWER

ENGINES.....15 to 250 H.P.....DETROIT DIESEL ENGINE DIVISION, Detroit, Mich.
ENGINES..750 to 2000 H.P...CLEVELAND DIESEL ENGINE DIVISION, Cleveland, Ohio
LOCOMOTIVES.....................ELECTRO-MOTIVE DIVISION, La Grange, Ill.

Above: This colorful magazine advertisement touts the horsepower delivered by the General Motors diesel engine that drives the M4 Sherman tank depicted in the combat scene. The M4A2 and M4A6 variants of the Sherman were manufactured with diesel powerplants. *Voyageur Press collection*

Right: Several members of an M4A1 Sherman tank crew sit idly while a young Belgian woman writes her name and a message with chalk on the hull of the armored vehicle. The M4A1 is distinguishable by its cast upper hull with a characteristic rounded silhouette. It appears that other young ladies have previously written on the tank's hull and that the activity is beginning to draw a crowd of civilians. The photo was taken in a Belgian town on September 8, 1944. *Voyageur Press collection*

the fuel trailer and the Americans contributing the M4 tank. Only four of these are known to have entered combat, supporting the 2nd Armored and 29th Infantry Divisions during their crossing of the Rhine River in early 1945.

The M4 chassis also served as the basis for mobile heavy artillery, including the 155mm Gun Motor Carriage M12 and its support vehicle, the Cargo Carrier M30, which transported additional ammunition for the gun. The 155mm gun of the M12 was based on the French GPF 155mm, and only one hundred of the M12 were completed during 1942 to 1943. A number of these were deployed to Western Europe and earned the nickname "Doorknocker" for their effectiveness against the fixed fortifications of the German Siegfried Line.

Opposite: Dated April 1, 1944, this overhead view of an M4A2 Sherman medium tank was taken at the Ordnance Operation Engineering Standards Vehicle Laboratory in Detroit, Michigan. This tank was built by Fisher and eventually deployed overseas. Along with the M4A6, the M4A2 Sherman variant was powered by diesel engines. The M4A2 utilized a pair of GMC 6-71 straight sixes. *US Army*

Right: Newly manufactured M4A2 Sherman tanks, mounting an early 75mm main weapon, sit aboard railroad flatcars for transport to a finishing depot. Five manufacturers completed more than eight thousand M4A2 Sherman variants between April 1942 and May 1944. *Voyageur Press collection*

Below: A quartet of M4A3 Sherman medium tanks executes a drill in the role of mobile artillery near the French village of La Cambe in August 1944. Several versions of the M4A3 were produced during World War II, and the tank was outfitted with wider tracks for more optimal distribution of weight. *US Army*

By 1945, the 155mm Gun Motor Carriage M40 had arrived on the Western Front in limited numbers. The M40 was built on the modified hull of the M4A3 HVSS, lengthened and widened to stabilize the gun platform. The M40 featured the "Long Tom" 155mm gun developed in the United States to replace the French GPF, and 418 were completed in 1945. Armed with the M115 8-inch howitzer, the Howitzer Motor Carriage M43 was constructed on the lengthened and widened chassis of the M4A3. Only forty-eight of these were completed, and the design was not standardized until November 1945, after the end of World War II. The M43 did serve with distinction during the Korean War. Both the M40 and M43 were products of the Pressed Steel Car Company.

The largest weapon ever considered for the M4A3 chassis was a ten-inch muzzle-loading mortar. In the spring of 1945, the Ordnance Committee of the US Army authorized a study of the tentatively named T94 Mortar Motor Carriage. The mortar shells were so heavy that a crane was required to load the weapon.

A wooden mockup was built, but the project was abandoned after World War II ended.

Late in the war, a fully outfitted M4A2 or other M4 variant was used on a limited basis as a platform for several early US-developed multiple-launch rocket systems. These included the T34 Calliope, which fired 113mm or 183mm rockets from up to sixty tubes; the T40/M17, which fired up to twenty 183mm rockets from an apparatus that could be jettisoned if necessary; and the later T99 with a pair of eleven-tube launchers on the sides of the turret.

From 1943 to 1945, the M4 chassis supported the development of at least twenty-six types of mine-clearing systems. Although some of these never progressed beyond the conceptual stage, the first operational version, using large front rollers that were extended to

During field exercises at Fort Drum, New York, in the 1950s, soldiers of the 42nd Infantry Division, New York National Guard, gather around a map table with an M4A3 Sherman medium tank in the background. The M4A3 was the only Sherman variant produced by Ford Motor Company, which manufactured nearly 1,700 from June 1942 through September 1943. *Department of Defense*

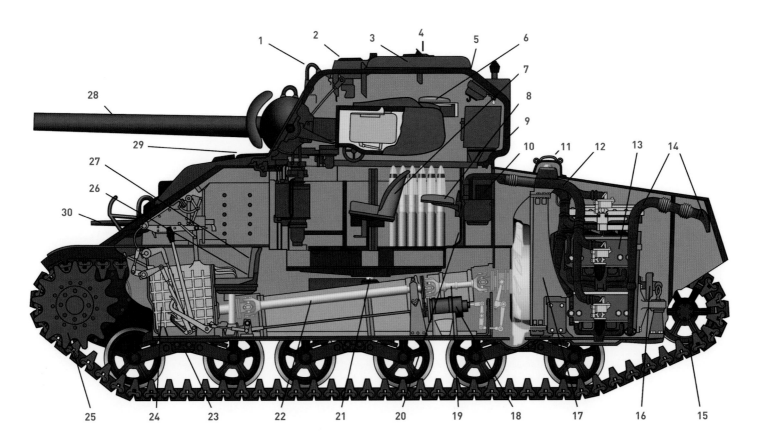

From July 1942 through November 1943, the Detroit Tank Arsenal completed 7,499 Chrysler-powered M4A4 tanks. This cutaway provides a fantastic view of major components: 1. Lifting ring; 2. Ventilator; 3. Turret hatch; 4. Periscope; 5. Turret hatch race; 6. Turret seat; 7. Gunner's seat; 8. Turret seat; 9. Turret; 10. Air cleaner; 11. Radiator filler cover; 12. Air cleaner manifold; 13. Power unit; 14. Exhaust pipe; 15. Track idler; 16. Single water pump; 17. Radiator; 18. Generator; 19. Rear drive shaft; 20. Turret basket; 21. Slip ring; 22. Front drive shaft; 23. Suspension bogey; 24. Transmission; 25. Main drive sprocket; 26. Driver's seat; 27. Machine gunner's seat; 28. 75mm gun; 29. Driver's hatch; 30. M1919A4 machine gun. *Malyczkz/Creative Commons 3.0*

detonate mines with ground pressure, was deployed in Italy in 1943. British designers developed the Sherman Crab flail tank, which used a rotating bobbin and forty-three lengths of chain to thrash the ground at 142 revolutions per minute, exploding buried mines in a swath ten feet wide at a speed of 1.5 miles per hour. The Sherman Crab was superior to other anti-mine tank designs because its flail was powered by the tank's main engine rather than an external engine that was more prone to breakdowns or damage.

Experimentation with amphibious apparatus resulted in the DD (Duplex Drive) Sherman, equipped with a canvas shroud that was watertight and could be raised while the tank was traversing water and then lowered to allow the tank to move forward and engage the enemy on land. A pair of small propellers was

fitted at the rear of the M4 and engaged to provide water-borne propulsion. Developed primarily for the D-Day landings, these tanks were initially conceived by Nicholas Straussler, a brilliant engineer who was born in Hungary in 1891 and immigrated to Great Britain between the world wars.

M4 tanks were sometimes fitted with deep wading gear, identified by the extended air ducts that were mounted externally on the exhaust system and engine ventilation hatches. With watertight hatches sealed, air was circulated one meter above the tank, allowing it to operate at depths approximating three meters. This system was used during amphibious landing operations and in the fording of rivers and streams. The T6 flotation system was adopted for the M4A2 in February 1944. Consisting of four pontoons fabricated as pressed

steel floats and welded to each side of the hull, the T6 system was used on a limited basis, most notably with the 1st Tank Battalion of the US Marines and other units during the invasion of Okinawa on April 1, 1945.

The M32 series of recovery vehicles utilized the M4 chassis with a sixty-thousand-pound winch and an eighteen-foot-long pivoting A-frame jib. This apparatus was sent forward to retrieve damaged tanks and other vehicles for repair and eventual return to the fighting. For use in the establishment of a defensive perimeter while the M32 was in action, an 81mm mortar was often placed within the confines of the open turret area. Initially based on the M4A1 chassis, modifications in the series

included the M32A1B1 with the HVSS suspension and the 81mm mortar removed to accommodate better retrieval equipment, and the M32B2 and M32B3 based on the chassis of the M4A2 and M4A3 respectively.

The M74 Armored Recovery Vehicle, an improvement on the M32 capable of handling heavier tanks of the post–World War II era, entered service in the early 1950s, and a few conversions of the M32B1 to the M34 Prime Mover for service as an artillery tractor were completed at the Ford Motor Company's Chester Tank Depot in 1944. The M35 Prime Mover was configured from the chassis of the M4A3 to tow 155mm or 8-inch artillery pieces.

For excavation, construction, and earth moving, the M4 chassis was commonly equipped with hydraulic bulldozer blades. An example of this is the M4 Dozer, fitted with a blade compatible with the Caterpillar D8 bulldozer. These were common sights during the construction of airfields, the clearing of jungle vegetation, and the digging of artillery emplacements in all theaters of World War II. The M4 Mobile Assault Bridge was one of several M4 configurations that carried or deployed temporary bridging equipment to expedite the movement of troops and equipment across streams. The T15, E1, E2, and several other variants of the M4 were evaluated with the anti-mine T14 package, consisting of reinforced tracks and thicker armor for the vulnerable underside of the tank, but canceled with the end of World War II.

Among America's World War II allies, Great Britain received by far the greatest number of M4 tanks:

Left, opposite, and following page: That the M4 Sherman became an iconic vehicle almost as quickly as it hit the battlefront is attested to by the scores of period print advertisements in which its recognizable lines were featured. *Zenith Press collection*

Below: This M4A2 Sherman of the 14th Armored Brigade, 2nd Polish Corps is depicted during the period of the Battle of Monte Cassino in May 1944. The red triangle is its squadron designation, and the camouflage scheme is still desert, consisting of olive drab spots on the sand backing. *Slawomir Zajaczkowski*

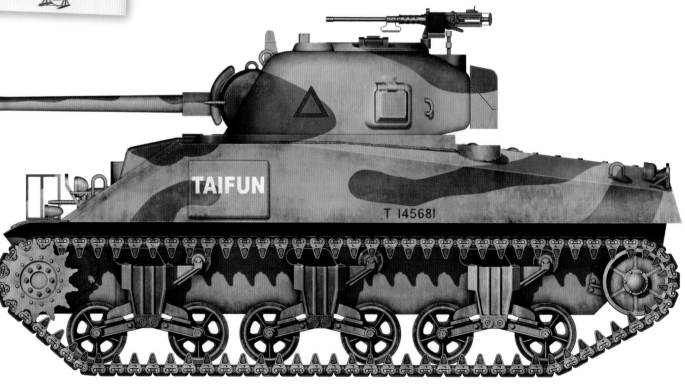

THE SATURDAY EVENING POST

BUY
WAR BONDS
TODAY
Keep America
Free

Victory pace *by Fisher*

GREAT masses of heavy armament are now helping to write the prologue to victory.

Fisher Body has produced its share of this armament—tanks, anti-aircraft guns, gun-breech housings, fighting planes, bombers and delicate flying instruments.

To do this we had to disregard the normal limits of our business, and build products entirely new to us. We had to explore technical fields foreign to us. We had to enlarge our plant facilities.

Looking back on those hectic days and nights of conversion, we realize that an understanding of true craftsmanship proved to be, literally, a lifesaver. Precision work on armament came easily to precision workmen. Long-acquired skills and crafts met demands for the most extreme accuracy.

And an impor[...] has yet to fail [...] manship has [...]

GENERAL MOT[...]

armament
BODY BY Fisher

DIVISION OF GENERAL M[...]

June 24, 1944

BUY
WAR BONDS
AND STAMPS
TODAY
Keep A[...]
Free

"Better than a rabbit's foot!"

Our fighting men have a tough job to do, and they are doing it.

They are finding out, in all parts of the world, what they have to work with. They are the best judges of the weapons with which American industry is supplying them.

They know just how fast the General Sherman M-4 medium tank will go — how accurate that seventy-five is — and whether or not direct hits will bounce off the armor plate.

The test of action in actual service gives them the final answer—the only one that matters.

Here at Fisher, we want to make sure it's the *right* an-

swer. That's why we give our tanks, bombers, and aircraft guns the best we've got in us. We're using e[...] craft we've mastered, every special skill we've devel[...] — and they add up to an impressive number — to [...] our armed forces that all-important edge.

Come the pinches, craftsmanship always counts. [...] it's only natural that our fighting men should rate such craftsman- ship as "better than a rabbit's foot."

First in the automo[...] for the Navy "E" s[...] Fisher has also been [...] Army-Navy "E" for [...] schedule tank produc[...]

armament
BODY BY Fisher

DIVISION OF GENERAL MOTORS

BETTER HOMES & GARDENS, APRIL, 1943

THE SATURDAY EVENING POST

BUY
WAR BO[...]
TOD[...]
Keep A[...]
Free

On every fighting front *Fisher*

THE men who do the fighting, wheth- er on land, sea or in the air, know how important it is to have the best equipment.

They realize that the work we do in our factories can, if done well enough, give them a combat advantage.

We realize that, too. That's why we are devoting all the skills we have devel-

oped, all the crafts we have mastered, to give our armed forces the all-important edge.

Whether it's a plane, an anti-aircraft gun, a tank, or a highly sensitive flying instrument, each gets every technical plus we can give it — and that's several.

Craftsmanship is a Fisher tradition. And today we believe craftsmanship carries a

The Army-Na[...] Fisher plant[...] production an[...] production, [...] four stars, in [...] plant for its in[...]

particular punch of[...] fighting man a brea[...] more than welcome.

GENERAL MOTORS SY[...]
NBC N[...]

armament
BODY BY Fisher

DIVISION OF GENERAL MOT[...]

approximately seventeen thousand representing about thirty-four percent of the total output from 1941 to 1945. The British were the first to use the M4 in combat, deploying more than 250 M4A1s stripped from US Army armored formations and rushed to the Eighth Army in Egypt prior to the pivotal Battle of El Alamein in October 1942. In keeping with their tradition, the British named the M4 after an American general of the Civil War era—this time Union Gen. William Tecumseh Sherman. The name stuck, and the M4 has been commonly known to history as the Sherman.

Like the other tanks and armored vehicles of the British Army, the Sherman variants in British service were identified as a series of Marks. The standard M4, therefore, was the Sherman I with the Continental R-975 engine and the 75mm M3 L/40

gun. The Sherman Hybrid I designated those that were manufactured with a composite hull, cast in the front and welded in the rear. The M4 mounting the 105mm infantry support howitzer was called the Sherman IB.

The Sherman MII was equivalent to the M4A1, while the Sherman IIA designated the M4A1(76)W and the Sherman IIAY matched the M4A1(76) W HVSS. The Sherman III was the basic M4A2, followed by the IIIA and the IIIAY matching the M4A2(76)W and the M4A2(76)W HVSS. The Sherman IV was equivalent to the M4A3 with the 75mm L/40 gun, while the Sherman IVA matched the M4A3(76)W, the Sherman IVB the M4A3(105), and the Sherman IVBY the M4A3(105) HVSS. The Sherman V was virtually the same tank as the M4A4 with the Chrysler multibank engine, while

Opposite: An M4A3 Sherman nicknamed "Hurricane" is pictured with Deep Wading gear installed. The ability to ford small streams and waterways gave the M4 great cross-country ability during World War II. The M4A3 was the first Sherman variant to be produced with horizontal volute spring suspension (HVSS) improvement. Note the US Army insignia atop the turret for easy recognition from the air. *US Army*

Above: Photographed in Germany in 1945, a Sherman "Crab" utilizes its rotating drum and chains. *Voyageur Press collection*

Left: A M4 Sherman Crocodile tank modified to carry a flamethrower spews fire at a target in Germany in September 1944. The Crocodile was one of many modifications made to the basic M4, including recovery and support vehicles, self-propelled artillery, and rocket-firing variants. Some of the most famous were conceived as DD (Duplex Drive) tanks that were mobile on both water and land. *US Army*

the Sherman VI was the British placeholder for any Canadian production, and the Sherman VII designated the M4A6. The Sherman II Armored Recovery Vehicle (ARV) was the M32B1 in British service, and the late–World War II Sherman V ARV III matched the M32B4, originally derived from the chassis of the M4A4. Few examples of the Sherman V ARV III are known to have existed.

As World War II progressed and the firepower and armor protection of German tanks increased, the British began their own program of upgunning the Shermans in their possession. Based primarily on the hulls of the M4A4 and the M4, the British modified nearly 2,300 Shermans during the war to carry the Ordnance QF 17-pounder gun, designed originally in 1941 to 1942 as an antitank weapon. A 76.2mm gun, the 17-pounder was a high-velocity gun that put the modified Sherman on par with the best German guns in terms of range and penetrating power.

The idea for the upgunned Sherman, nicknamed "Firefly," began with the development of the latest generation of British cruiser tanks, the Cromwell and the A30, which became the Challenger. While the Cromwell mounted the Ordnance QF 75mm gun, the Challenger was fitted with the 17-pounder. Two officers who were assigned to the A30 project at Lulworth, Lt. Col. George Witheridge and Maj. George Brighty,

Below: This 1944 image captured during the Italian Campaign depicts a valuable modification to the standard M4 Sherman tank. The attachment of a bulldozer blade allowed engineers to work even while under enemy fire, and Gen. Dwight D. Eisenhower praised the innovative dozer tank in his book *Crusade in Europe. Voyageur Press collection*

Opposite: An anti-mine M4 "Crab" utilizes its system of chains and rolling drums during a demonstration of its capabilities. Adept at clearing minefields, the Crab was one of many innovations that utilized the M4 chassis. *FPG/Getty Images*

Outfitted with a roller apparatus that performed numerous functions, an M4 medium tank advances across a snow-covered landscape as a crewman observes the armored vehicle's progress. A variety of specialized attachments were developed for use with the M4. *Voyageur Press collection*

both experienced tankers, pushed for the modification of the Sherman to accept the 17-pounder even after the suggestion was initially rejected.

Modifying the Sherman turret to accommodate the 17-pounder was not a simple task; however, Vickers engineer W. G. K. Kilbourne was instrumental in the success of the project. The existing Sherman turret was too small to house the 17-pounder's lengthy recoil. One suggested solution, the removal of the recoil system completely, would have required the entire tank to absorb the shock of firing the weapon and eventually shaken the vehicle apart.

Among other alterations, the successful modification of the Sherman turret involved adding a welded box to its rear. After live-fire trials were concluded in December 1943, the first Fireflies were converted to carry the 17-pounder in January 1944. By midyear, nearly 350 conversions had been completed,

and the ever-quickening pace resulted in 268 conversions in the month of September alone.

On the battlefields of Western Europe, German tank crews soon became aware of the lethality of the Firefly, easily recognizable since the 17-pounder's barrel was significantly longer than those of other contemporary British tank guns. A single Firefly was usually assigned to a troop of four tanks, and the Germans sought to disable or destroy the Firefly first and then engage the more lightly armed Shermans that remained.

Other British and Canadian modifications included the Sherman Tulip, equipped with a pair of sixty-pound, three-inch RP-3 rockets on rails affixed to the turret and used by the Coldstream Guards during the Rhine Crossing in the spring of 1945; the Skink, carrying quad-mounted 20mm Polsten antiaircraft cannon on the Grizzly hull; the Kangaroo armored

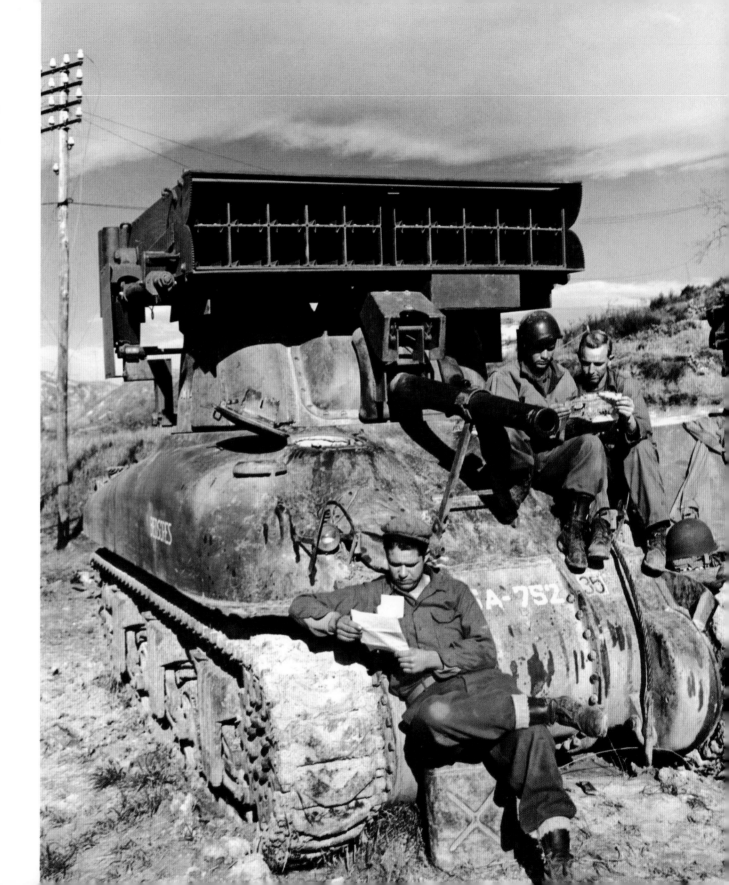

Three American soldiers relax on the chassis of an M4 Sherman tank modified to carry a multiple launch rocket system and renamed the Rocket Launcher T-40, or "Whizbang." One of the soldiers is apparently reading a letter from home while the others read a newspaper. *Voyageur Press collection*

personnel carrier; bridge-laying variants; and the Beach Armoured Recovery Vehicle (BARV), a converted Sherman III capable of operating in comparatively deep water near the shoreline.

Several of these modified Shermans were at least partially associated with the innovative mind of British Maj. Gen. Percy C. S. Hobart, commander of the 79th Armoured Division, which developed and deployed a collection of specialized tanks, primarily derived from the British Churchill and the American M4 Sherman. Collectively, this group of tanks was known as "Hobart's Funnies," and the most prominent of its novelty machines was the DD Sherman. British Army engineers took Straussler's early concept, adapted it to the Sherman, and conducted field tests at Staines Reservoir in Surrey near London. The DD was the only "Funny" that

senior US commanders chose to utilize during the D-Day landings.

Remembering his introduction to the DD Sherman that his unit would soon be issued and trained to operate, Lt. W. D. Little of the Canadian Fort Garry Horse Regiment commented, "This little barge turned and headed toward us, and as it rolled you could see it struck the bottom of the pond or lake, and started to roll up. Lo and behold, tracks! This was a tremendous surprise. Then as it rolled forward, the tracks kept coming higher; and then as it got to the edge of the water, down came the screen and there was the gun. This was a terrific surprise and shock."

Virtually all of the more than four thousand Shermans sent to the Soviet Union via Lend-Lease were M4A2s, evenly divided between those mounting 75mm and 76mm guns. The Soviets reportedly

Top left: A multiple launch T34 rocket system attached to the chassis of an M4 Sherman medium tank sets loose a deadly barrage of explosive missiles somewhere in France during World War II. The versatile M4 chassis appeared in numerous configurations during the war. *US Army*

Top right: An American soldier with the US Army's 101st Airborne inspects an abandoned British M4 Firefly during Operation Market-Garden in September 1944. German tank crews soon became aware of the lethality of the upgunned Firefly, easily recognizable by its 17-pounder's barrel. *US Army*

The crew of a British M4 Sherman Firefly medium tank, easily distinguished by the length of its 17-pounder gun, rests momentarily during operations in the Belgian city of Namur in the autumn of 1944. The introduction of the 17-pounder gave the Firefly a weapon with enough muzzle velocity to effectively knock out German tanks with increased armor protection. *Voyageur Press collection*

The *Fury* Tank

The feature film *Fury*, starring Brad Pitt, won critical acclaim following its release in 2014, and the primary reason is its realistic depiction of combat during World War II.

Pitt stars as a battle-hardened tank sergeant in command of an M4A3E8 Sherman tank, the famed Easy Eight, assigned to hold a vital crossroads against a battalion of SS soldiers during the Allied drive into Germany late in the war. The film accurately depicts the combat that takes place between a platoon of Easy Eights and a single German PzKpfw.VI Tiger tank.

The action in *Fury* also relates the experience of a tank crew performing assigned tasks within the confines of the hull and turret of a Sherman tank and coping with the emotional stress associated with the rigors of wartime service. For those who seek a realistic, true-to-life perspective on the ordeal of the American tank soldier in World War II, *Fury* offers quite probably the best portrayal to have come along thus far.

Japanese poster for the film *Fury*. *Voyageur Press collection*

---

modified some M4A2 models to carry the M1940 F-34 76mm gun common to the legendary T-34 medium tank.

Along with the armored units of the Free French armed forces, the M4 Sherman also equipped military formations from numerous other nations during World War II. The 4th New Zealand Armoured Brigade fielded about 150 examples of the M4A2 and experienced heavy combat during the Italian Campaign from 1943 until the war's end. Chinese forces received more than eight hundred Shermans during the course of the war, and many of these continued in service during the civil war that followed between the Nationalists under Chiang Kai-shek and Communist forces led by Mao Tse-tung.

The Polish II Corps, which gained fame in Italy, utilized the M4A2. The Polish 1st Armored Division was equipped with the M4A1 and other variants, and the British supplied the Czech 1st Armored Brigade with a complement of Firefly tanks during the fighting in France. A total of eighty-three Sherman tanks were delivered to Brazil for home defense during and after World War II. Many of these were in use with the country's military until the 1970s.

After World War II ended, the M4 Sherman remained in service in various configurations with the armies of numerous nations, including Israel, Egypt, Pakistan, Jordan, Saudi Arabia, Australia, the Philippines, and scores of others, while modifications of the proven chassis continued for many years.

Opposite left: South of the village of Vaucelles, France, Canadian tankers pause to rest during the Normandy Campaign in June 1944. The M4 Sherman that these tankers operate was a primary armored fighting vehicle of the Canadian Army in World War II. *Library of Congress*

Opposite right: The 1970s movie *Kelly's Heroes*, starring Clint Eastwood, combined World War II action with postwar countercultural sensibilities. Both German and American tanks— including the M4—play prominent roles in the fanciful scheme to steal Nazi gold. This poster touts the Danish release of the film. *Voyageur Press collection*

CHAPTER SIX

On the World War II Battlefield

The news was profoundly shocking. The fortress city of Tobruk had surrendered, and twenty-five thousand British soldiers were captured. When he received the news on the night of June 20, 1942, British Prime Minister Winston Churchill was meeting with President Franklin D. Roosevelt in Washington, DC.

Sensing the gravity of the situation, Roosevelt offered assistance. Churchill thought for a moment and then asked for all the tanks the Americans could spare. The showdown in North Africa was coming, and the British Eighth Army was in dire need of tanks, guns, and other war materiel. The scene of the decisive battle of the North African Campaign was an obscure railroad whistle stop near the Egyptian-Libyan frontier known as El Alamein. East of the line where the British stood was the Egyptian capital city of Cairo, the great

port of Alexandria, the Suez Canal, and the oilfields of the Middle East. For the British, further defeat was unthinkable.

During the Battle of El Alamein, October 23 through November 4, 1942, the British, under Gen. Bernard Law Montgomery, did in fact defeat the Axis Panzerarmee Afrika led by the legendary Gen. Erwin Rommel. However, it was near-run thing. One of the deciding factors between victory and defeat was the arrival of the first American-built Sherman tanks to see combat during World War II.

In response to Churchill's request, Roosevelt and Army Chief of Staff Gen. George C. Marshall contemplated sending the fully equipped US 2nd Armored Division, under Maj. Gen. George S. Patton Jr., to Egypt; however, it was determined that the logistical

With an M4 Sherman tank following in support during the Battle of El Alamein, British infantrymen advance past the smoking hulk of a German PzKpfw. III tank and an abandoned 88mm gun in this oil-on-canvas by William Francis Longstaff. The deployment of the M4 at El Alamein gave the British Eighth Army significantly enhanced armored capability during the pivotal battle in the North African desert. *National Army Museum, London via Bridgeman Images*

challenge was too great. Shipped without the troops and other equipment, the vital tanks would reach the Eighth Army more quickly. British crews could take them into battle. Roosevelt, therefore, ordered the assembly of a small convoy in New York Harbor to be swiftly loaded and sail at high speed for the Middle East.

Factory-fresh M4A1 Sherman tanks were shipped by rail car to New York. Meanwhile, according to some sources, other supplies and equipment were loaded on the waiting ships prior to the arrival of the tanks. The freighters *Zaandam*, *Tarn*, *Exhibitor*, *Empire Oriole*, and *Hawaiian Shipper* were already fully loaded when the M4A1s arrived. Some accounts say that the entire initial allotment of M4A1s totaled eighty-three and that all

were loaded aboard the *Fairhope*. Others state that the tanks were distributed among more than one of the freighters. Regardless, with a small escort, the convoy embarked on the hazardous voyage on July 13.

Three days later, five hundred miles north of the Virgin Islands, the German submarine U-161 struck the *Fairhope* with two torpedoes. The freighter sank within ten minutes. Miraculously, no lives were lost, but the *Fairhope's* complement of new tanks had gone to the bottom of the Atlantic.

When word of the sinking of the *Fairhope* reached Washington, DC, arrangements were quickly made to replace the losses. More tanks of both the 1st and 2nd Armored Divisions were shipped by rail to New

The M4 Sherman rode to the rescue in North Africa in 1942. This tank's crew used mud as makeshift "camouflage" over the customary olive drab, which was a bit dark for the environs. *Slawomir Zajaczkowski*

Canadian war artist Charles Fraser Comfort completed this surreal watercolor depicting an M4 Sherman tank in a nocturnal air raid. The silhouette of the M4 is unmistakable; however, the tank did not make its combat debut until the Battle of El Alamein in October 1942. *Canadian War Museum via Bridgeman Images*

York and loaded aboard the freighter *Seatrain Texas*, which undertook the hazardous voyage across the Atlantic, around the Cape of Good Hope, and to the southern end of the Suez Canal virtually alone. Again, accounts vary as to how many M4A1s the *Seatrain Texas* carried. The true number probably lies between 52 and 250. The freighter left New York on July 29, took on fuel and provisions at Cape Town, South Africa, picked up an escorting corvette off the port of Durban, avoided an Italian submarine in the narrows off the coast of Italian Somaliland, and reached Port Taufiq on September 2.

A single M4, christened the Sherman by the British after American Civil War–era Gen. William

Tecumseh Sherman, had been sent to Egypt in early August so that Eighth Army troops might at least become somewhat familiar with the American tank. By September 11, the number of Shermans—both M4A1s and possibly a few diesel-powered M4A2s—totaled 318. Their arrival had been kept top secret, and throughout their transport and deployment the Shermans were known by the code name "Swallow." The new tanks were hurriedly repainted and equipped for desert warfare with the addition of blanket boxes attached to the turret bustle, sand shields, and rails along the flanks that could support sun shields for the crew when bivouacked. British radios were installed.

On the eve of the Battle of El Alamein, 252 Sherman tanks were with the forward elements of the Eighth Army, deployed among approximately a dozen armored units, including the 2nd Dragoon Guards; 9th Queen's Royal Lancers; 10th Hussars; Yorkshire Dragoons; Nottinghamshire Yeomanry; 41st, 45th, and 47th Royal Tanks of the 24th Armoured Brigade; and 3rd Hussars, Royal Wiltshire Yeomanry, and Warwickshire Yeomanry of the 9th Armoured Brigade. The thirty-six Shermans of the 9th Armoured Brigade reached the front line only hours before the Battle of El Alamein began.

The Shermans bolstered the Eighth Army's complement of Crusader, Valentine, M3 Grant, and M3 Stuart tanks, and their baptism of fire came as a rude shock to the Germans and Italians, whose own strength in tanks had steadily dwindled during months of combat as Allied interdiction by air and sea strangled Axis supply lines across the Mediterranean Sea. The Sherman's 75mm main gun was adequate to deal with the German PzKpfw. III and PzKpfw. IV tanks manufactured by the Germans during the early war years and superior to the Italian M13/40 and Semovente tanks.

Known as the Bays, the 2nd Dragoons Guards went into battle at El Alamein alongside the 10th Hussars. Following a tremendous preparatory artillery barrage, the Bays lost three Shermans to mines before sunrise on October 23. Shortly after daylight, a troop of Shermans destroyed an antitank gun, but then two more were lost to mines. Later that morning, the Shermans of the Bays's B and C Squadrons advanced with infantry protecting their flanks, Australians to the north and the Gordon Highlanders to the south, and A Squadron and the 10th Hussars in support to the rear. The British

When the United States entered World War II, its armed forces lacked personnel, equipment, and training. As the nation geared up for war, the M4 Sherman tank was rushed to the production line. In this photo taken in October 1942, American tank soldiers train with their M4s in the desert of California. *National Archives*

Shermans pitched into more than twenty German tanks and several antitank guns, destroying half the enemy tanks in a swirling fight.

The following day, the Bays joined the 9th Queen's Royal Lancers to fend off a German counterattack. Shermans and Crusaders slugged it out with the Germans, and twenty-six enemy tanks were destroyed. At least two more British tanks were lost to mines, and as night fell on October 24 only twelve of the Bays's original twenty-nine Shermans were still operational. Eleven replacement Shermans were brought up on the 25th, and the Bays and Lancers attempted to support troops manning 6-pounder antitank guns at Outpost Snipe. These gallant men were essentially marooned, and when the Shermans topped the crest of nearby Kidney Ridge their high silhouettes drew heavy German fire.

The Bays lost five Shermans and the Lancers eight during the fighting at Outpost Snipe, but the Germans had felt the impact of the Sherman. Before withdrawing from the position, the British infantry and artillerymen, along with the Shermans and Crusaders of the Bays and Lancers, had destroyed or damaged at least thirty-three German tanks. Estimates of German losses in the heavy fighting at Outpost Snipe run as high as fifty-three tanks.

Above: In North Africa, British tankers used an inventive camouflage scheme consisting of olive drab "waves" overlapping a sand-colored hull with a thick white line painted between. This M4A1 served with the 3rd Armoured Brigade at the Battle of El Alamein. *Slawomir Zajaczkowski*

Opposite: An American M4 Sherman tank raises a thick cloud of dust as it races across the North African desert during the Battle of El Guettar in 1943. The action at El Guettar was the first major victory of American ground forces against the German army during World War II. *Eliot Elisofon/The LIFE Picture Collection/Getty Images*

The first Sherman tanks deployed with American troops against the Germans came ashore during Operation Torch, the Allied invasion of North Africa, on November 8, 1942. The inexperienced American troops learned hard lessons in North Africa against Rommel's combat veterans, and the most costly of these was during the Battle of Kasserine Pass in February 1943. The Germans attacked the US 1st Armored Division positions stretched thinly along a sixty-mile front, their workhorse PzKpfw. IV tanks and new PzKpfw. VI Tigers slashing deeply into rear areas, isolating large numbers of American soldiers while others abandoned weapons and equipment and fled in disorder.

Around noon on February 14, the first day of fighting, fifty-one Shermans of the 3rd Battalion, 1st Armored Regiment counterattacked the Germans, losing forty-four tanks in a savage encounter but slowing the enemy advance. During a counterattack the following day, two platoons of Shermans from the 2nd Battalion, 1st Armored Regiment overran several German antitank positions, destroying four 88mm and two 47mm guns and killing fifty enemy soldiers.

One Sherman reached the edge of the small village of Sidi Salem and promptly knocked out two enemy tanks. Other enemy vehicles were set afire as the American tanks took control of the town. West of Sidi Salem, a platoon of Shermans surprised four PzKpfw. IVs and blasted two of them. Another pair of German tanks was knocked out near the same location a short time later. One Sherman platoon accounted for eight enemy tanks during the melee, while a single Sherman was cornered by seven German PzKpfw. IVs and managed to destroy one of them before it was blown apart.

Within minutes, however, the situation changed. American intelligence had estimated that only forty German tanks were in position to oppose the attack. Actually, more than one hundred were in the vicinity, while well-placed artillery and antitank gun positions were prepared to meet the advance of the inexperienced American tankers. Swiftly, the trap was sprung.

One company of fourteen German tanks advanced to a low hill that commanded a level plain that the

Left: Great Britain's King George VI inspects a line of US M4 Sherman Mk IIIs in North Africa in June 1943. *US Army*

Right: A crew tests an M4 Scorpion mine-clearing tank in North Africa sometime in 1943. *US Army*

Americans would have to cross if they continued to move forward. From the south, twenty-five more PzKpfw. IVs moved up. The Americans were soon engaged from both the front and flank. Armor-piercing 75mm and 88mm shells tore through the thin armor of the Shermans.

Lieutenant Colonel James D. Alger, commander of the 2nd Battalion, realized he was in trouble just as a German round crashed into the engine compartment of his command tank, setting it on fire. Two more German shells struck the turret in rapid succession, killing the radio operator. Alger and the surviving members of his crew were taken prisoner.

When it was over, the 2nd Battalion had been virtually destroyed. During two days of hard fighting, the 1st Armored Division had lost ninety-eight tanks, scores of vehicles and artillery pieces, and at least five hundred killed, wounded, or captured. Eventually, stalwart defenders and the superb handling of the

Above: Humphrey Bogart starred in the 1943 Hollywood film *Sahara*, which depicted the wartime trials and tribulations of tank soldiers battling the Nazis in North Africa during World War II. Interestingly, while the poster depicted an illustration of an M4, the actual film used an M3 as Bogart's vehicle. *Voyageur Press collection*

Right: Published in *Look* magazine, this stylized account of fighting in the North African desert tells the story of an American M4 Sherman tank crew that fought a heroic engagement against long odds. Taking on ten enemy tanks, the crew destroyed four of them and then rescued a large number of Allied infantrymen. *Voyageur Press collection*

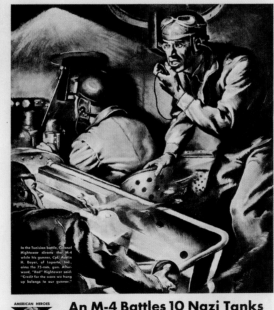

9th Infantry Division artillery stopped the German offensive at Kasserine.

The Americans gained combat experience in North Africa at a terrible price. Two months after the Kasserine debacle, elements of the II Corps under General Patton stood toe to toe with the German 10th Panzer Division at the Battle of El Guettar. The fight ended in a draw, but the performance of the American tanks and troops was vastly improved.

When the Allies landed on the island of Sicily on July 10, 1943, senior commanders were well aware that armored operations might be limited due not only to stubborn German and Italian resistance, but also to the rugged terrain. However, the American beachhead at Gela was quickly challenged when German tanks of the Hermann Göring Division and Italian mechanized units of the Livorno Division and Mobile Force E counterattacked.

In response, elements of the 2nd Armored Division were hurried ashore from the Seventh Army floating reserve. The soft sand caused problems, and the Shermans of Combat Command B (CCB) had a tough time getting off the beach. As the enemy attack moved forward the next morning, the Germans came close to smashing the American lodgment.

When Maj. Clifton Batchelder of the 3rd Battalion, 67th Armored Regiment asked Col. Isaac White, commander of CCB, how he planned to deal with the

An M4A1 of E Company (hence, "Eternity"), 2nd US Armored Division as it appeared during the Allied invasion of Sicily in July 1943. This Sherman appears to retain vestiges of the sand-colored paint used in the previous North African campaign. *Slawomir Zajaczkowski*

While Fifth and Eighth Army forces desperately attempt to crack the stubborn German defenses of the Gustav Line in Italy, an M4 Sherman tank rumbles across a temporary bridge erected during the heavy fighting around the town of Cassino. *George Rodger/The LIFE Picture Collection/ Getty Images*

Opposite: Free French soldiers rest in a poppy field alongside their M4 Sherman tanks during a break in their movement toward the front line during the Italian Campaign. Another vehicle that made a great contribution to the Allied victory in World War II, the 2½-ton truck, is visible in the center of the photo. *George Silk/The LIFE Picture Collection/Getty Images*

Right: Painted in a rather unique camouflage scheme, an M4 Sherman tank in service with the British Eighth Army pauses along a road in Italy in 1943. These tankers have nicknamed their armored vehicle "Sheik." *Voyageur Press collection*

threat, White responded, "Plans hell! This may be Custer's last stand!"

Four Shermans under Lt. James White finally moved forward and hit the Germans in the right flank. Heavy shells from the US Navy cruisers *Boise* and *Savannah* and concentrated artillery fire weighed in to stop the enemy advance.

The mountainous landscape of Italy also proved less than ideal for mechanized operations, and much of the bloody Allied slog up the Italian boot was marked by the desperate reach of the Fifth and Eighth Armies for good "tank country." While British landings took place further south, the Americans hit the Italian mainland on the beaches of Salerno on September 9, 1943. The landing was hotly contested, and again the Germans came close to driving the Americans into the sea. During a half-hour of fighting on September

14, a single tank destroyer of the 636th Battalion knocked out five German tanks and a truck filled with ammunition. Sherman tanks and every artillery piece that could be scrounged joined in to eliminate a total of thirty German tanks that day.

During the Italian Campaign, Allied mechanized forces were limited in their mobility to the few good roads and highways and the broad plains that stretched from the banks of rivers, while adverse weather conditions often restricted operations as well. The German defenders regularly occupied strong defensive lines that stretched from the Tyrrhenian Sea in the west to the Adriatic in the east, and tank versus tank encounters were somewhat rare. However, the firepower of the Sherman and the British Churchill were welcome as their 75mm and 76mm guns were effective against fortified enemy positions and troop concentrations.

ATTIC

General Dwight D. Eisenhower, commander of Allied forces in the Mediterranean Theater, reflected on the arduous Italian Campaign in his postwar memoir *Crusade in Europe* and noted that the Sherman tank was particularly adaptable. As German troops executed a brilliant fighting withdrawal, they destroyed any facilities that might be of use to the advancing Allies, blew up bridges, and detonated explosives to cause landslides that blocked roads.

"To restore these to some semblance of usefulness we had to use the ever-present bulldozer," Eisenhower wrote. "They had to work with, sometimes even in front of, our front lines in order that necessary supplies could be brought up to the troops and wounded could be evacuated."

"The enemy countered this by hidden machine guns and other long-range, light-caliber weapons, which, from the safety of a thousand yards' distance picked off operating personnel and often destroyed the machines themselves. Some imaginative and sensible man on the home front, hearing of this difficulty, solved the problem by merely converting a number of Sherman tanks into bulldozers. These tanks were impervious to all types of small-arms fire and could not be destroyed except by shells from a large-caliber gun or by big mines. From that time on our engineering detachments on the front lines began to enjoy a degree of safety that actually led them to seek this kind of adventurous work. None of us could identify the individual responsible for developing this

Above: A Sherman from A Company ("Attic"), 13th Armored Regiment, US Army, as it appeared when landing at Anzio in April 1944. Brown began to complement olive drab in camouflage schemes, and the white beneath the barrel was intended to disperse the shadow. The three red rectangles signify 3rd Platoon. *Slawomir Zajaczkowski*

Opposite: This M4 Sherman tank was destroyed by enemy fire during the battle for the town of Cassino, Italy. Much of the Italian terrain was less than ideal for armored operations, and Allied tanks often fell victim to mines or concealed antitank weapons that the Germans placed along narrow roadways. *Carl Mydans/The LIFE Picture Collection/Getty Images*

piece of equipment but had he been present he would have, by acclamation, received all the medals we could have pinned upon him."

As World War II in Europe progressed, the versatility of the Sherman tank became apparent, while its shortcomings were laid bare. The Sherman was simple and reliable and required only basic field maintenance. It was relatively easy to mass produce and therefore available in large numbers. Its power-traverse turret could rotate in a 360-degree arc much more quickly than enemy tanks, allowing the Sherman to acquire targets and fire rapidly, and its interior was spacious. It was fast and maneuverable. During the fighting in Italy, reports of the Sherman in action in the mountainous terrain reached the highest echelons of the German command structure.

In his memoir *Inside the Third Reich*, German Armaments Minister Albert Speer commented, "On the southwestern front (Italy) reports on the cross country mobility of the Sherman have been very favorable. The Sherman climbs mountains which our tank experts consider inaccessible to tanks. One great advantage is that the Sherman has a very powerful motor in proportion to its weight. Its cross-country mobility on level ground (in the Po Valley) is, as the Twenty-Sixth Armored Division reports, definitely superior to that of our tanks. . . ."

In sharp contrast, German tanks were overengineered and prone to breakdowns, and their weight—particularly in the case of the Tiger—sometimes strained their powerplants beyond reasonable endurance. Although there is a persistent consensus that the Sherman could outmaneuver the most modern German tanks, the Panther was capable of making the pivot turn in its own space, keeping its main weapon and frontal armor directed toward the enemy. The Sherman, however, was required to move either forward or backward to turn.

While the inadequacies of the Sherman's short-barreled 75mm gun in armored combat are well known, other aspects of the tank's performance presented early problems. The tank's high silhouette did indeed offer a prominent target for enemy

On the road to the famed Italian city of Pisa, home of the great Leaning Tower, a tank crew of the American 752nd Armored Battalion keeps watch at an important road junction. The commander has positioned his M4 Sherman tank to take advantage of partial concealment offered by a pile of rubble. *PhotoQuest/Getty Images*

gunners, particularly while traversing prominent terrain features, and restricted its effectiveness fighting from a hull-down position. The Sherman's armor was deemed inadequate to defend against high-velocity German munitions, and often tank crews resorted to appliqué armor, sandbags, tires, chicken wire, or other materials to augment their protection.

The Sherman tank was also prone to catching fire, or "brewing up," when hit by an enemy shell. This was particularly true of the early models. Initially, this phenomenon was attributed to the gasoline engines that were prevalent and the high-octane fuel that they consumed. On closer examination,

though, it became apparent that the dry storage of ammunition in sponsons above the tank tracks was a major contributing factor. As wet ammunition storage was introduced, the tanks became less susceptible to a catastrophic explosion in the event of a hit.

Still, even with the introduction of wet ammunition storage in the M4A1, the Sherman's reputation for brewing up persisted. Allied soldiers began referring to the tanks as "Ronsons," alluding to a popular cigarette lighter of the period that advertised its reliability with the slogan "Lights up the first time, every time!" German soldiers began calling the tanks "Tommy Cookers," in reference to the nickname of the British

On February 1, 1944, American Gen. Dwight D. Eisenhower, Supreme Commander Allied Expeditionary Force (center), and British Deputy Supreme Command Air Chief Marshal Sir Arthur Tedder (far right) observe maneuvers in the English countryside while standing with the crew of an M4 Sherman tank. *Frank Scherschel/The LIFE Picture Collection/Getty Images*

soldier, Tommy, and a field stove that was widely used by British troops in the trenches of World War I. Other Lend-Lease Shermans received similar unflattering monikers. Polish tankers referred to them as the "five-man cremation device," and Russian troops called them the "burning grave."

Still, it must be remembered that American armored doctrine overshadowed the development and construction of the Sherman tank. Large numbers of tanks that would be used for exploitation would serve a fast-moving, offensive army well in the field, while the open-turreted tank destroyers would engage and defeat enemy tanks. Even as the British introduced their superb 17-pounder gun with the Sherman and converted a substantial number to their Firefly configuration, the military establishment in the United States—primarily Gen. Lesley McNair, chief of the Army Ground Forces—remained staunchly opposed to the idea of a heavy tank.

In November 1943, an Army Ground Forces policy statement reached the following conclusion.

"The recommendation of a limited proportion of tanks carrying a 90mm gun is not concurred in for the following reasons: The M4 tank has been hailed widely as the best tank on the battlefield today. . . . There appears to be no fear on the part of our forces of the German Mark VI (Tiger) tank. There can be no basis for the T26 tank other than the conception of a tank-vs.-tank duel—which is believed to be unsound and unnecessary."

The assertion that American tank crews had no fear of the German Tiger is astonishing. If they did not fear it, American Sherman crews certainly respected the Tiger. The allusion to the T26 tank is indicative of the heated debate that raged within the upper echelons of the army command structure during 1943 to 1944, particularly the Army Ground Forces, the Ordnance Department, and those senior officers who grasped the evolving nature of combat in Western Europe, acknowledging that tank versus tank combat was inevitable and that a heavier tank was needed. Others, as the policy statement reflects, vehemently disagreed.

In late 1944, an agreement was reached that authorized the production of 250 T26 tanks with increased armor protection and a powerful 90mm main gun. The first of these reached the 3rd and 9th Armored Divisions in Europe in January 1945, but only twenty of the tanks served in combat. By the spring of 1945, the heavy tank had been standardized as the M26 Pershing and about two hundred had been deployed to Europe.

Several factors influenced the delay in production of the Pershing. American factories were already fully geared up for the Sherman and producing it in large numbers. Logistics challenges, particularly supply lines that stretched thousands of miles across the Atlantic, dictated that heavy weapons that had not been tested in battle were impractical from a transportation perspective. The parity of the early Sherman with second-generation German tanks fostered a sense of

Part of the Operation Fortitude deception prior to D-Day, dummy M4s made completely of rubber fooled the Germans into believing that the Allies were massing forces for an attack at the Pas de Calais rather than Normandy and that the fictitious First US Army Group (FUSAG), under Gen. George S. Patton Jr., would lead the invasion. *National Archives*

Undoubtedly posing for the photographer, the crew of an M4 gazes toward the coast of France during maneuvers conducted somewhere in the English countryside on February 17, 1944. Four months later, Allied armored units were fighting the Nazis in the hedgerows of Normandy. *H. F. Davis/ Getty Images*

Apparently the victim of a German mine or artillery shell, an M4 has been blown onto its side and abandoned in Normandy in June 1944. The brutal fighting in the hedgerow country took a heavy toll on the M4 tanks; however, the armored vehicles were instrumental in exploiting the subsequent Allied breakout and dash across France. *Ullstein Bild/Getty Images*

complacency among some senior army commanders, slowing the development of a new tank. Finally and foremost, the Tank Destroyer Doctrine prevailed.

General Jacob Devers, commander of the Armored Force from August 1941 through May 1943 and later commander of the VI Army Group in Western Europe, was a tireless advocate of the development of heavier tanks. Although McNair agreed to the upgunning of the Sherman with the 76mm weapon, he staunchly opposed further commitment of resources to the T26.

In the autumn of 1943, McNair wrote to Devers, "The M4 tank, particularly the M4A3, has been widely hailed as the best tank on the battlefield today. There are indications that the enemy concurs in this view. Apparently, the M4 is an ideal combination of mobility, dependability, speed, protection, and firepower. Other than this particular request—which represents the British view—there has been no call from any theater for a 90mm tank gun . . . . Both British and American battle experience has demonstrated that the antitank gun in suitable number and disposed properly is the master of the tank. Any attempt to armor and gun tanks so as to outmatch antitank guns is foredoomed to failure. . . . There is no indication that the 76mm antitank gun is inadequate against the German Mark VI (Tiger) tank."

Controversy dogged the Sherman during World War II and continued even after McNair was killed by errant Allied bombing during Operation Cobra, the Allied breakout from Normandy, in July 1944.

During the course of World War II, the US Army fielded sixteen armored divisions. The composition of these divisions was revised on more than one occasion. In the autumn of 1943, the standard armored division was reorganized from two tank regiments to three tank battalions, each of these with a supporting battalion of armored infantry. The 1st and 2nd Armored Divisions, already cohesive fighting units, were exempted from the reorganization and remained "heavy" armored divisions through the end of the war.

The reorganization was initiated to reduce the number of tanks organic to the armored division and the number of personnel from more than 14,000 to about 10,500. The number of midlevel commanders was reduced, while the complement of armored infantry was augmented. Such organization clearly supported the concept of combined arms with armor and infantry supporting one another as the circumstances of battle dictated. The division included five elements: command, support, service, reconnaissance, and striking. The armored division included its headquarters and three combat commands: designated Combat Command A, Combat Command B, and Combat Command R (reserve). Each combat command included one tank and one infantry battalion along with specific support formations and was considered capable of operating for a period of time as a self-sustaining task force.

The 1943 US tank battalion included a headquarters company with assault gun and reconnaissance platoons, three companies of medium Sherman tanks, and a single company of Stuart light tanks. Tank companies were comprised of three platoons of five tanks each, while two tanks were assigned to the headquarters section. A single M4(105) howitzer was assigned to each medium tank company.

The sternest test of the US Armored Force and the Sherman tank in World War II was yet to come—with the invasion of Normandy on June 6, 1944. Aside from the noted exceptions, the newly formed US armored divisions that fought their way across France, into Germany, and to victory in Western Europe were organized to the new standard.

Allied strategic and tactical planning for the opening of a second front against Nazi-occupied Europe was underway as early as 1942, and the buildup of men and materiel transformed the villages and countryside of southern England into a massive armed

camp. Once Normandy was chosen as the site for the D-Day invasion, which took place on June 6, 1944, tactical considerations turned to the establishment of a beachhead that could be rapidly expanded and withstand the inevitable German counterattack that would likely include a significant commitment of enemy tanks and armored vehicles.

D-Day planners recognized that getting armor onto the invasion beaches—designated Sword, Juno, Gold, Omaha, and Utah, stretching fifty miles from east to west along the Norman coastline—was a key to early success. Tanks could blast enemy strongpoints and spearhead the drive inland while also providing

The village of Caen in Normandy was a D-Day objective that was not captured by the Allies for nearly a month after the landings. Strong German opposition resulted in some of the most savage fighting of the Normandy Campaign and the loss of many M4 Shermans. In this photo, the crew of a camouflaged British Sherman prepares to move out during operations to capture Caen. *Galerie Bilderwelt/Getty Images*

Shermans in Soviet Service

The United States supplied 4,102 M4 Sherman medium tanks to the Soviet Red Army through Lend-Lease during World War II. Virtually all of these were the diesel-powered M4A2 variant. Their numbers were divided evenly between those armed with the original short-barreled 75mm gun and the high-velocity 76mm gun version, which began to arrive in the Soviet Union in the early autumn of 1944.

By the end of the war, the Red Army had actually designated some units, including the 1st, 2nd, and 9th Guards Mechanized Corps, to be equipped exclusively with the M4A2, although the vaunted T-34 and upgunned T-34/85 medium tanks were in adequate supply in 1944 to 1945.

The Soviets referred to their Sherman tanks with the nickname "Emcha," a reference to the Cyrillic letter "Cha," which resembles the Arabic numeral "4" with an open top in the M4 designation. The diesel M4A2 was less prone to catching fire than gasoline-powered Soviet tanks, and the Sherman received mixed reviews with the Red Army. Colonel Dmitriy Fedorovich Loza commanded Sherman tanks during the Great Patriotic War, as the Soviets called World War II, and praised its performance, although he did advise that the M4A2 was better suited for "colonial" campaigns rather than all-out war.

Loza fought across Eastern Europe from the Ukraine to Hungary and Austria. He also commanded Soviet T-34s and British Matilda tanks before his unit, the 1st Battalion, 233rd Tank Brigade, 5th Mechanized Corps, received its first Shermans in the autumn of 1943. In September 1944, the unit was redesignated the 46th Guards Tank Brigade, 9th Mechanized Corps. Loza was seriously wounded in combat with a German PzKpfw. VI Tiger tank but survived the war to retire from the Red Army in 1967. For valor during heavy combat in the vicinity of Vienna, Austria, he was designated a Hero of the Soviet Union.

One of Loza's most memorable battles aboard the M4A2 Sherman occurred in the central Ukraine in January 1944, while he served as chief of armaments for the 1st Battalion, 233rd Tank Brigade. After Soviet forces had stopped a German attack, a tank company under the command of Lt. Georg Avakovich Chobanyan spent the winter night in the open.

"The night passed quietly," Loza remembered. "The nervous company commander was at his post early in the morning. The sky was white, and snow continued to fall. The Shermans were white hillocks. . . . Chobanyan looked around at the southern slope of the hill on which his company

This reproduction of an original color photograph shows M4 Sherman tanks of the Soviet Red Army advancing through a city on the Eastern Front. Behind the two M4s is a self-propelled gun. *Voyageur Press collection*

stood. He blinked his eyes in disbelief. Below him some four hundred meters, blanketed in the same snow covering, stood seven or eight German Tiger tanks. . . . What now?

"Georg Avakovich climbed up to awake the crew of the closest Emcha. . . . Quickly explaining the situation to them, he showed them the enemy tanks that could be discerned on the terrain. . . . Chobanyan's company began hurried preparation to commence firing. . . . The air was clear. The targets were not sharp, but they were visible just the same. It was time for a salvo. Fire!

"Two Tigers went up in flames. On the remainder, the turret hatches began to clank open. The enemy tankers, awakened in ignorance from their sleep, twisted their heads around searching for the firing enemy tanks. The second Sherman salvo gave them their final wake-up call. Three more Tigers were set afire. There were no answering shots. Taking advantage of the smoke screen from burning Tigers, undamaged vehicles were hurrying in the direction of Pavlovka.

"The Emchisti celebrated. In such an unbelievable situation that had arisen out of pure chance, they had found themselves the victor."

the firepower needed to counter enemy armor. The challenge lay in getting the tanks ashore under fire, and the disastrous raid on the French port of Dieppe in August 1942, during which numerous British Churchill tanks had foundered in shallow water and failed to negotiate the loose sand and pebble-strewn beach, had underscored the difficulty of such an endeavor. For the Normandy invasion, codenamed Operation Overlord, the Duplex-Drive (DD) Sherman offered the best option to accomplish the task.

Ten battalions of DD Shermans were assembled for D-Day, and these were to be released from landing craft approximately two miles off the invasion beaches and make their way to shore under their own power. Heavy rains and the worst spring weather in half a century postponed the invasion for twenty-four hours, and by the time the landing craft carrying nearly one hundred thousand infantrymen had turned toward the beaches on June 6, 1944, winds still whipped the waters of the English Channel.

The release of the DD Shermans was risky business, but it went forward with the rest of the assault. Eight tanks failed to reach the shore at Gold Beach, swamped in heavy seas. DD tanks of the 7th Royal Dragoon Guards and the Sherwood Rangers Yeomanry plowed ahead and took on German machine gun nests and bunkers.

In this chilling photograph, a single M4 is seen advancing through the bocage, or hedgerow country, of Normandy from the vantage point of a German observation post. Often, the Allied tanks were ambushed by well-concealed German antitank guns or individual soldiers with shoulder-fired weapons such as the Panzerfaust. *Ullstein Bild/Getty Images*

German soldiers seem to be enjoying the ride aboard a captured M4. Well known for recycling captured arms and putting them to use with their own forces, the Germans did deploy some Sherman tanks late in World War II, particularly as their own weapons were destroyed and available numbers dwindled. *Voyageur Press collection*

At Juno Beach, the Canadian 7th Infantry Brigade and twenty-one of the twenty-eight DD tanks of the 1st Hussars moved off the beach rapidly. The rough seas prevented some of the DD tanks from reaching the shore during the early landings, and these were offloaded later directly onto the beach. Tank gunner Earl Kitching of the Fort Garry Horse remembered his early moments at Juno Beach.

"We started from about a mile offshore," said Kitching, of Stony Mountain, Manitoba, "and it took us about an hour to get onto the beach. This was our first time in battle, and while we had confidence in our machines, we did not know what we might be walking into. We had never lost an amphibious tank in training, but here we ran into complications, the rough water, mines, and obstacles. Of the twenty in our troop, seven were lost, probably swamped. One tank was disabled on the beach but repaired the following day. Twelve of us made it to shore and moved inland."

Above: Ready to button up and roll forward to the attack at a moment's notice, crewmen aboard an M4 Sherman tank sit at the line of departure near the town of Reffuveille, France, in July 1944. *Photo 12/Getty Images*

Opposite: Equipped with blades on its forward hull to cut through the imposing hedgerows of Normandy, an M4 Sherman crests a rise, briefly exposing its vulnerable underside in the direction of the enemy. Infantrymen accompany the tank during its advance toward the French village of Saint-Sauveur-le-Vicomte. *US Army/The LIFE Images Collection/Getty Images*

Lieutenant Bill Little of the Fort Garry Horse ordered his tank down the ramp of a Landing Craft, Tank (LCT) and into the water. German bullets whizzed by his head. "A tank commander always has to have his head up," remarked Little, "and that's how Sergeant P. Parkes, my troop sergeant, and his operator, Lance Corporal Stevenson, were killed. Both shot by sniper fire. . . . And Sergeant Spud Murphy, a shell hit his tank and down it went. . . ."

By late afternoon, the Canadian infantry of the North Shore Regiment and the DD tanks of the Fort Garry Horse had silenced several German strongpoints at Juno Beach and forced the enemy

troops occupying the troublesome Tailleville Chateau to surrender.

Elements of the American 4th Infantry Division were slated to land at Utah Beach. However, the strong current pushed the assaulting troops into the wrong area. Undaunted, Col. James Van Fleet and Brig. Gen. Theodore Roosevelt Jr., son of the famed American president, decided to start the war from their current position rather than divert forces to the original landing zone. At 5:47 a.m., LCT 597 struck a mine and sank immediately. Its load of four DD Shermans went to the bottom of the channel without firing a shot. An officer aboard another vessel observed, "We were but

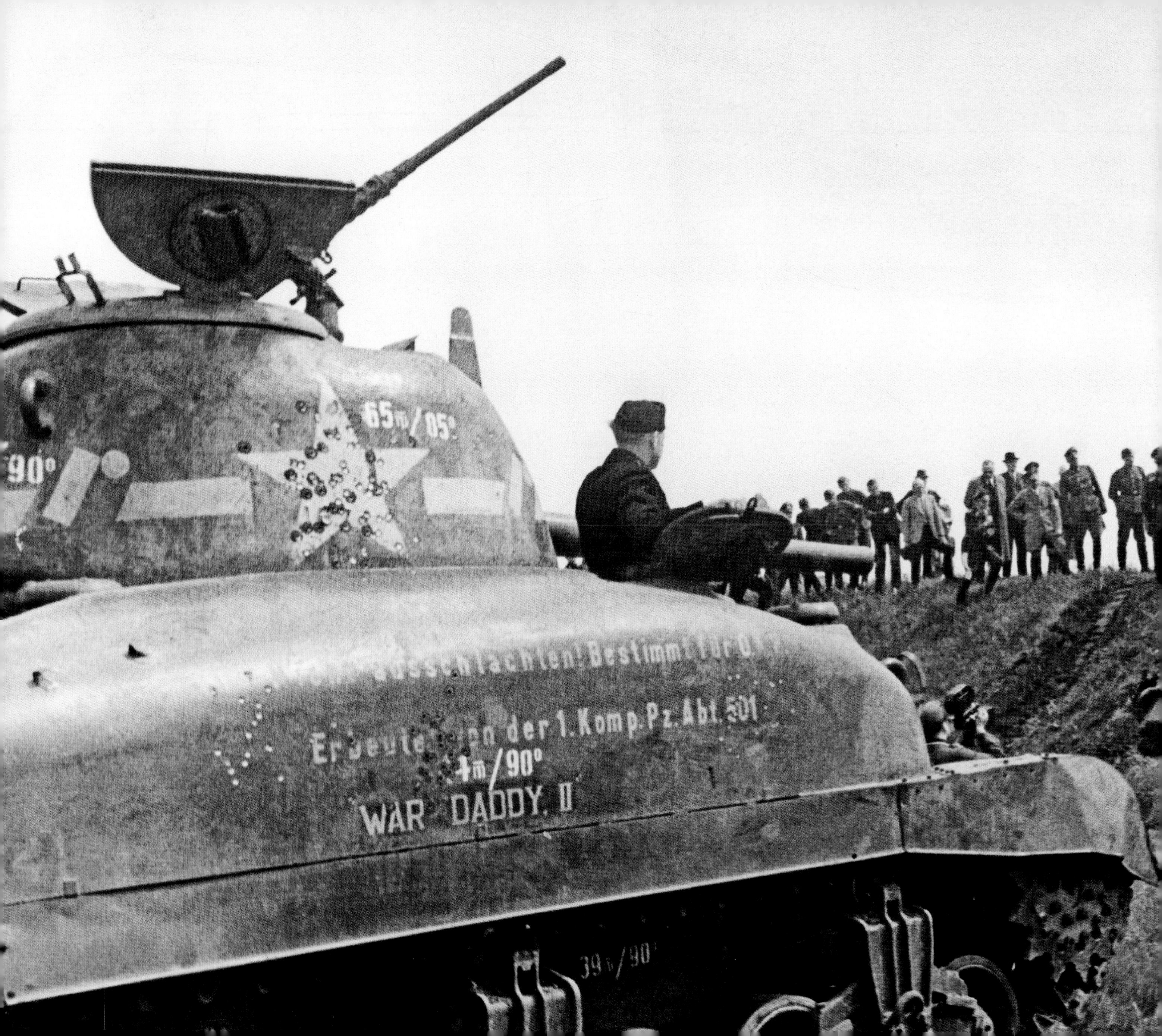
ausschlachten! Bestimmt
der 1. Komp. Pz. Abt. 501
WAR DADDY. II

A captured American M4 Sherman tank (foreground) is ready to be put through its paces before an audience of German officers on July 1, 1944. The performance of the M4 is being compared to the PzKpfw. V Panther medium tank (background) of German manufacture. Overall, the Germans were impressed with the M4's reliability and cross-country mobility. *Ullstein Bild/Getty Images*

a few yards away and felt the explosion's potent shock waves course through our craft."

Nevertheless, twenty-seven tanks did come ashore on Utah Beach and engage the enemy during the push inland.

Units of the US 1st and 29th Infantry Divisions hit Omaha Beach, where the German 352nd Infantry Division manned strong fortifications. As soon as they came into range, the American landing craft came under heavy, accurate fire. The situation was in doubt until mid-morning, and at one time Gen. Omar Bradley, commander of US ground forces during Operation Overlord, considered withdrawing the troops and diverting subsequent landings to sectors that were less hazardous. Countless acts of bravery and supporting naval gunfire turned the tide at Omaha Beach; however, casualties were extremely high.

The ordeal of the DD tanks off Omaha Beach contributed to the difficulties encountered by the troops landing there. Sixty-four DD Shermans were allocated to the 741st and 743rd Tank Battalions, and due to the heavy German fire the twenty-nine tanks of the 741st Battalion were launched into roiling waters three miles from the shore. Twenty-seven of these foundered and sank, many of their crewmen drowning inside.

From his vantage point aboard LCT 535, Navy Lt. Dean Rockwell commanded a flotilla of LCTs off Omaha Beach. He watched in horror as the flotilla to his left launched its tanks offshore and all but three of the thirty-two sank immediately. Rockwell broke radio silence and contacted Capt. Ned Elder, commander of C Company, 743rd Tank Battalion. The two agreed that the tanks assigned to the Dog White and Dog Green

sectors of Omaha Beach should be landed directly on the sand.

As the commanders of the surrounding LCTs ordered their throttles opened, some of the Shermans began firing at German positions from the decks of the vessels. Rockwell ordered the ramp of LCT 535 lowered, and four DD Shermans waddled into three feet of water fifty yards from shore. Rockwell remembered, "We pulled that famous naval maneuver, known through naval history as getting the hell out of there."

Amazed that his large LCT, lying sideways to the position of an 88mm cannon, had not immediately drawn withering German fire, Rockwell watched the tanks open up with their 75mm guns. As the gray light of dawn began to streak the sky, the infantrymen of the 116th Regiment, 1st Division were headed toward the uncertain shore.

Although Allied forces were unable to achieve all of their D-Day objectives, as the sun set on June 6, 1944, it was apparent that they were on the European continent to stay. There were numerous reasons

The commander of an M4 Sherman rides in the open hatch of his vehicle through the streets of a shattered village in Normandy sometime in 1944. Although the M4 was inferior to German tanks in single combat, it was readily available and reliable. In the end, it overwhelmed enemy armor by sheer weight of numbers. *Universal History Archive/ Getty Images*

Right: Photographed near the town of Ohlungen, France, in 1944, crewmen replenish the ammunition stock aboard this M4 Sherman tank. Note the improvisation of sandbags added to the turret and chassis of the vehicle to augment existing armor protection. The muzzle of the tank's 76mm gun is capped while the M4 is withdrawn from combat. *Voyageur Press collection*

Bottom: Pictured on August 2, 1944, is the M4 Sherman tank "Romilly," the first French-manned tank to enter Paris during the liberation of the City of Light. The crew was primarily Republican refugees of the Spanish Civil War. The tank's commander, Adjutant Henri Caron, is not pictured. He was later killed in action. *Voyageur Press collection*

for their success, not the least of which was the contribution made by those tanks, particularly DD Shermans, that managed to reach the invasion beaches early in the fighting.

An unexpected benefit to the Allied effort on D-Day was the disagreement among senior German commanders regarding the deployment of powerful panzer divisions to Normandy. Rommel, commander of the Atlantic Wall defenses, wanted to bring German armor close to the shore to repel an invasion on the beaches. His superior, Field Marshal Gerd von Rundstedt, commander of German forces in the West, advocated holding the tanks a distance from the Channel coast to strike a decisive blow once the Allies were fully ashore. Operation Fortitude, an elaborate Allied deception, kept the Germans off balance. Many senior German officers expected the invasion to

come further north at the Pas de Calais. Thus, Hitler retained direct control of the panzer reserves and did not release them to Normandy in time to seriously threaten the Allied lodgment.

The only appreciable German armored force to counterattack on D-Day included elements of the 21st Panzer Division, which reached the coastline at Lion-sur-Mer, temporarily driving a wedge between British forces on Sword Beach and the Canadians at Juno Beach. The drive met stiff resistance from both infantry and tanks, and eventually the Germans were compelled to withdraw for lack of reinforcements.

The following day, the Canadian 27th Tank Regiment, Sherbrooke Fusiliers, and infantry of the North Nova Scotia Highlanders took on PzKpfw. IVs and Panzergrenadiers of the 12th SS Panzer Division Hitlerjugend. In the fierce battle, twenty-eight Shermans were lost, and fifteen PzKpfw. IVs were destroyed.

One of the key British objectives on D-Day was the communications and transportation center of Caen. The Germans held tenaciously to Caen for six weeks, seriously disrupting the Allied timetable in Normandy. During

Operation Goodwood, July 17 to 20, the British 7th and 11th Guards Armored Divisions and the 3rd and 51st Infantry Divisions battled the 12th SS Panzer Division Hitlerjugend and the 21st Panzer Division. Both sides took heavy casualties, the 11th Guards Division losing 126 tanks and armored vehicles. Both German divisions were mauled during the fighting in Normandy, losing scores of tanks to Allied armor and tactical air strikes.

Along with the stiff German defense, the land itself was a prominent adversary to the Allied effort. The hedgerows, or bocage, were long ridges of earth with drainage ditches running alongside that stretched for miles between pastures and farmlands in Normandy. The hedgerows were centuries old and usually several feet thick with trees growing up to twenty feet high on top of them. The natural formations of the bocage made for excellent defensive terrain.

The Germans concealed tanks, machine guns, antitank weapons, and snipers in ambush positions throughout Normandy, and the narrow dirt roads between the hedgerows became death traps. The cost of a single day's advance was often measured by the

Top left: The versatile M4 chassis was modified for a variety of combat and support roles during World War II. This Sherman belonging to Gen. George S. Patton's Third Army in France mounts a multiple launch rocket system that was capable of bringing heavy fire on a concentrated area. The T34 variant of the M4 was nicknamed "Calliope" due to the sound of its rockets discharging. *Voyageur Press collection*

Top right: Another view of an M4 Calliope. The later T34E1 Calliope was distinguishable by the fact that its four groups of rocket-launching tubes each comprised 14 tubes, an upgrade from 12 as seen in this initial version. *Voyageur Press collection*

Opposite: In the summer of 1944, American forces liberated the town of Domfront, France. In this image, an M4 probes its way across a bridge through a shattered village on the road to Domfront, attesting to the fact that at times in order to liberate a town it was necessary to destroy it. *Photo12/Getty Images*

Above: Soldiers of the US 3rd Infantry Division inspect an M4 Sherman that has apparently been disabled by a mine somewhere in France. This M4 belonged to the 756th Tank Battalion, which took part in Operation Dragoon, the invasion of southern France on August 15, 1944, and the heavy fighting in the Colmar Pocket in early 1945. *Voyageur Press collection*

Opposite: On August 15, 1944, Maj. Gen. George "Pip" Roberts (right), commander of the British 11th Armoured Division, confers with Brig. Roscoe Harvey, commander of the 29th Armoured Regiment, in front of the latter's M4 Sherman command tank. This conversation took place while the division was engaged in heavy fighting in France. *IWM/Getty Images*

dead and wounded it took to sometimes gain but a few hundred yards. Armored vehicles were more or less restricted to the confines of the country lanes and became easy targets for hidden German weapons.

While a few Sherman dozer tanks were available to cut through the thick hedgerows, Sgt. Curtis G. Culin of the US 102nd Cavalry Reconnaissance Squadron, 2nd Armored Division is credited with the idea of welding steel blades to the front hulls of Sherman tanks and M10 tank destroyers. Some sources state that Culin acted on the suggestion of another soldier; however, the implements are today known as the "Culin Hedgerow Cutters," or more popularly as "Rhino Devices," and the tanks that sported them were fittingly referred to as "Rhino Tanks" because of these tusk-like appendages.

The primitive plow-like Culin Cutters allowed the tanks to push through the mounds of earth without exposing their thinly armored undersides to enemy fire. Hundreds of American tanks were modified with

the appendages, and British engineers used scrap metal to modify many of their tanks as well. German obstacles cleared from the D-Day invasion beaches supplied some of the steel used to make the blades.

During the fight for Caen, British tanks of the 4th Armoured Brigade and infantry of the 43rd Wessex Division fought elements of three German panzer divisions, the 10th SS Freundsberg, 9th SS Hohenstaufen, and 12th SS Hitlerjugend, for control of a commanding position called Hill 112, named for its height in meters.

Tank gunner Ken Trout remembered the excitement and fear of fighting in the hedgerows. "'Driver, advance!'" he wrote. "The Sherman climbs up the bank. I get a view of the treetops above the hedge. We level off and stay perched on the bank. This is the evil moment when the Sherman shows its thinly plated bottom to any gunner or bazooka man sitting in the field beyond. It is a naked, unprotected feeling. Hickey revs the engine a little, we begin to topple, a giant hand seems to rip the hedge aside, we crash down to earth and are through!"

Trout recalled that his Sherman advanced only a short distance in the bocage before encountering another hedgerow. "We roll up to the opposite hedge, merely a couple of rotations of our tracks and we are again pressing into the greenery. The commander must be able to see something from up above. . . . I sit and wonder whether the end of our barrel is projecting through the hedge to the amusement of a crew of German antitank gunners on the other side. . . . The leaves fall away from the periscope and I can see. Germans! By the next hedge. But dead. Lying in a group face downwards as though thrown there by some mighty blast. I point my guns at them. . . . As we begin to cross this further field, Rex calls, 'Those Jerries aren't dead!'"

The Germans that Trout and his fellow tankers encountered threw up their hands and surrendered. They were ushered toward the rear under the guns of accompanying British infantrymen. Other Germans, however, leaped to their feet and began running across the field to a concealed ditch.

In the autumn of 1944, the Allied forces in Western Europe were nearing the end of an impressive advance toward the German frontier. This American M4 Sherman tank of the 5th Armored Division rolls through the streets of a town in the Grand Duchy of Luxembourg that September. *Tony Vaccaro/ Getty Images*

"A German hops across the gate space like a scared rabbit," Trout wrote. "I am too astonished to react. Another German runs across the space, left to right. I douse the right-hand hedge with machine gun bullets. A third German takes the leap. . . . I am waiting for the fourth German with his basin-shaped helmet, his wide, neat tunic, his sloppy, baggy trousers, his carbine in hand. . . . 'Gunner, there's obviously a trench behind that hedge! . . . Operator, reload with HE. Gunner, fire three rounds of HE in your own time!' Tommy slaps my leg. I tread hard.

"The flame at the gun and the flame at the hedge are almost simultaneous. The hedge is so near that the tempestuous concussion against the hedge rebounds and slams the turret whilst the gun is still recoiling from its own discharge. . . . Another tornado. Slap. Tread. Blast. The hedge, what is left of it, begins to burn."

While engaging the infantry, Trout's Sherman crew was always wary of enemy tanks and the ever-present threat of the Panzerfaust, a shaped-charge, shoulder-fired antitank weapon. "Until now my main fear has been the elephantine shape of a heavy German tank, a Tiger, Panther, Royal Tiger, or self-propelled gun suddenly appearing downwind of us, its all-destroying gun pointing at us and its armor plate impervious to our 75mm shot," reflected Trout. "Now a new peril is evident. If single German infantrymen can pop in and out of ditches within fifty yards of our tank, single German infantrymen may be crawling through the hedges alongside us or through the long grass behind us.

"And some of those infantrymen carry the notorious Panzerfaust . . . an innocuous-looking instrument but one which, at fifty yards range, can blow our turret to smithereens. The cozy little fields darken into a tight, ugly deathtrap, as though a vast, black cloud had come

over the summer sun. We sit and watch the burning of the hedge and wonder about Panzerfausts."

The lethality of the German Tiger and Panther tanks required the Allies in their Sherman, Cromwell, and Churchill tanks to adopt innovative tactics to deal with the enemy armor. For example, a single Tiger or Panther might tie up as many as two platoons of four or five Allied tanks each during a sharp fight. Due to the greater range of the German guns, a platoon of Shermans often sought to close the range with the enemy tank, occupying the German crew while at least one of the other platoons or sometimes a single Sherman attempted to get behind a Tiger and fire a shot at its most vulnerable rear. Both the flanks and rear of the Panther were susceptible to the Sherman's 75mm or 76mm guns if an Allied tank could reach an advantageous firing position. Often enough, at least a couple of Shermans were lost in the fight.

During the summer of 1944, the Americans and British coped with their lack of firepower in tank versus tank encounters as best they could. According to the multivolume history titled *United States Army in World War II*, popularly known as the "Green Book Series," hard lessons were learned on the battlefield.

"The 2nd Armored Division tankers had learned how to fight German Panther and Tiger tanks with their M4 Shermans," the history reads. "They knew that the ammunition of the 75-mm. gun with which most of the M4s were armed (a low-velocity shell about 13 inches long, as compared with the 28- to 30-inch high-velocity 75-mm. shell of the Panthers) would not penetrate at any range the thick frontal armor of the Panthers and Tigers, but could damage the sides and rear. Therefore the tankers had used wide encircling movements, engaging the enemy's attention with one platoon of tanks while another platoon attacked from the rear. They had suffered appalling losses: between 26 July and 12 August, for example, one of 2d Armored Division's tank battalions had lost to German tanks and assault guns 51 percent of its combat personnel killed or wounded and 70 percent of its tanks destroyed or evacuated for . . . repair. But by using flanking tactics and by enlisting artillery support to fire directly on

Top left: Corporal Carlton Chapman, a machine gunner of the 761st Tank Battalion, peers through the hatch of an M4 Sherman tank near Nancy, France, on November 5, 1944. At the time, the primarily African American battalion was attached to a motor transport unit. The 761st Tank Battalion fought with distinction in Western Europe during World War II and received the Presidential Unit Citation. *National Archives*

Bottom left: A British M4 rolls across a bridge at Eindhoven, the Netherlands, during Operation Market-Garden in September 1944. The failed Allied operation was an attempt by Field Marshal Montgomery to enter Germany by circumventing the Siegfried Line, requiring the capture of bridges across the Maas and Rhine rivers, as well as several smaller waterways and canals. *US Army*

Opposite: Partially camouflaged by tree branches its crewmen have place on and around it, an M4 of the 1st French Army fires on a German position near the town of Belfort in northwestern France on November 20, 1944. Infantrymen crouch behind the tank as it fires at the enemy. *Photo 12/Getty Images*

enemy tanks, the Americans had won their battles and even managed to inflict heavy losses on the Germans.

"By the time the Roer offensive began [in November 1944]," it concluded, "the 2nd Armored Division's firepower had been stepped up to some extent. About half the division's M4s were armed with the 76-mm. gun. With this gun, firing the new but scarce tungsten-carbide-cored HVAP ammunition, the tankers could penetrate the front belly plate of the Panther at 300 yards and at 200 yards had a sporting chance (about one to four) of penetrating the front slope plate."

Lieutenant Colonel Albin F. Irzyk, commander of the 8th Tank Battalion, Combat Command B, 4th Armored Division, survived two wounds during World War II and was awarded the Distinguished Service

Cross and two Silver Stars among numerous other decorations. His army career spanned thirty-one years, and he retired with the rank of brigadier general after two tours of duty in Vietnam.

Among Irzyk's most vivid wartime memories of World War II were scenes he happened upon just after the breakout of Allied forces from the hedgerow country of Normandy during Operation Cobra. In an open field, he encountered the shadowy hulk of a tank. As he drew closer, he noticed the black cross emblazoned on the turret and saw that the tank's interior had burned thoroughly. Hit by a single round on its right flank near the front glacis, the tank must have immediately erupted in flames. Overcome with curiosity, Irzyk climbed atop the turret and looked inside. The charred bodies of

Left: Tankers of the US First Army's 5th Armored Regiment gather around a fire in a snow-covered field near the town of Eupen, Belgium, to open Christmas packages in December 1944. These soldiers have stretched a tent half from the flank of their M4 Sherman tank to provide some shelter against the elements. *US Army*

Opposite: A platoon of M4 Sherman tanks sits in a French field covered in snow that had fallen during the previous night. The rugged Sherman proved capable of operating in the harshest of conditions during the Allied drive across France and into the Third Reich in the waning months of World War II in Europe. Although the Sherman was at a disadvantage against heavier German tanks in single combat, its reliability and availability in great numbers provided an edge for the Allies. *National Archives*

A pair of Shermans from the US Army's 191st Tank Battalion fire on sniper-infested buildings in the center of Aschaffenburg, Germany, on April 2, 1945. *National Archives*

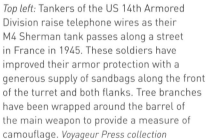

two crewmen were sitting upright, just as they had been moments before the fatal shot.

A short time later, Irzyk came across another disabled enemy tank situated on the edge of a treeline with its 75mm gun pointing toward a clearing and another wooded area. This was a Panther that had been knocked out but had not burned.

Then Irzyk caught a glimpse of five apparently intact Sherman tanks lying abandoned some distance away. On closer inspection, he was shocked to find that each tank had been disabled by a single shot—aimed directly at the large white star on the hull that marked them individually as American. Externally, with the exception of the single telltale hole that must have come from the Panther's 75mm gun, the tanks looked pristine.

The young officer gleaned a couple of valuable lessons from the experience. First, the white stars were highly visible targets, making the job of the German gunner easier. Along with other officers, Irzyk passed the word. The white stars on the turrets and hulls of the American tanks were to be muted with a wash of olive drab paint, mud, or anything else that might do the job. Second, if there was a sixth tank, it was the lone survivor and likely the Sherman that worked its way around to a vulnerable area to deliver the shot that destroyed the Panther. The American tankers had apparently ignored much of their stateside training. Although they had closed the range to the Panther, they had bunched up. They were almost on the same line and had not staggered their formation. Rather than maneuvering from different directions, they had

This rocket-firing M4 Sherman tank is in action on March 10, 1945, in support of a unit building a bridge across a waterway in Western Europe. The concentrated firepower of the rockets suppressed enemy fire against the American engineers who were working on the bridge. *AFP/Getty Images*

rolled forward together. The German gunner had picked them off with little difficulty and minimal traverse of his high-velocity gun.

The tactical deployment of the Sherman tank in Western Europe was the key to its success or failure on the battlefield. Operation Market-Garden, the ill-fated offensive of September 17 to 27, 1944, was conceived by Field Marshal Montgomery to capture bridges across waterways in the Netherlands with airborne troops. The British XXX Corps would execute a timely ground thrust across the spans followed by a plunge into the Ruhr, the industrial heart of Germany, possibly ending the war by Christmas.

Market-Garden resulted in a costly failure.

Aside from the fact that the air-ground timetable was ambitious, accurate intelligence reports that German armor was in the area of Market-Garden operations were discounted. The lightly armed paratroopers of the American 82nd and 101st Airborne Divisions, and particularly the British 1st Airborne at the town of Arnhem on the Lower Rhine, encountered much heavier resistance than anticipated. The XXX Corps was obliged to travel a narrow road to link up with each successive bridgehead, and each time resistance was encountered its tanks and accompanying infantry were required to deploy to dispose of the threat.

British Shermans and other armored vehicles were often silhouetted against the horizon while advancing on the road, making excellent targets for German antitank guns and Panzerfausts. On the afternoon of June 21, a pair of Sherman Fireflies of 4 Troop, C Squadron, 44th Royal Tank Regiment, proceeded along a country lane near

the Dutch town of Sint-Oedenrode. The tankers were expecting support from paratroopers of the 101st Airborne's B Company, 502nd Parachute Infantry Regiment. However, miscommunication left the tanks advancing on their own—right into an ambush.

Troops of the German 59th Infantry Division had prepared a roadblock and were manning a 75mm or larger-caliber weapon. The lead tank advanced about two hundred yards, and the German gun fired. The tank's driver was killed instantly, and the Firefly careened into a tree along the side of the road. The tank commander tried to extricate a wounded crewman from the disabled vehicle, but a second shot blew him off the tank. One wounded man staggered out of the Firefly and managed to limp approximately one hundred yards before German rifle or machine gun fire cut him down. The commander and other crewmen escaped. The second Firefly was also hit but withdrew under its own power.

The knocked-out Firefly remained wedged against the tree, which was chewed up by German machine gun bullets, for some time. Dutch villagers later buried the two dead British soldiers. Tanks and infantry were mutually supportive in theory and in practice. One advancing without the other in close proximity often made a deadly business even deadlier.

Laden with infantrymen and sandbags to augment the protection of their armor, American M4 Sherman tanks pause in the German village of Heppenheim on March 27, 1945. Within weeks, World War II in Europe was over as the German high command surrendered to the Allied Expeditionary Force in a schoolhouse in Reims, France. *Ullstein Bild/Getty Images*

The African American crew of an M4 Sherman prepares to go into battle in Germany during the final days of World War II in Europe. Although the US military remained segregated through the end of the war, African American tankers served with conspicuous bravery. *William Vandivert/The LIFE Picture Collection/Getty Images*

South of the Market-Garden fighting, Allied and German roles were reversed and the largest tank battle of World War II in Western Europe with the exception of the Battle of the Bulge occurred from September 18 to 29. In the French province of Lorraine, the German Fifth Panzer Army mounted an offensive against the US 4th Armored Divisions, and the resulting Battle of Arracourt ended with an American victory.

The German 111th and 113th Panzer Brigades were equipped with factory-fresh Panther tanks, and

the total strength of the Fifth Panzer Army included more than one hundred of these along with seventy-five PzKpfw. IVs. The replacement Panthers were fine tanks, and they were superior in firepower to the American Shermans. However, their crews were hurried into service with little training. Compounding the Germans' problems at Arracourt was a pronounced lack of reconnaissance capability.

Combat Command A of the 4th Armored Division included elements of the 37th and 35th

Tank Battalions, the 10th and 53rd Armored Infantry Battalions, the 66th and 94th Armored Field Artillery Battalions, the 25th Cavalry Squadron, the 704th Tank Destroyer Battalion, the 191st Field Artillery Battalion, the 166th Combat Engineer Battalion, and the 24th Armored Engineer Battalion. Although the Germans were numerically superior in tanks, the Americans were experienced. They fought from prepared defensive positions and held the edge in tactical air support. Bad weather temporarily concealed the Germans from air attack but also obscured their own visibility in battling the concealed Americans.

As the Germans advanced, the Battle of Arracourt degenerated into a series of repeated armored thrusts that the Americans blunted with superior tactics. On the morning of September 19, for example, a company of the 113th Panzer Brigade breached the thin line of Combat Command A on two sides. A company of Shermans and two tank destroyer platoons flanked the German Panthers and Mark IVs and destroyed eleven of them while M7 Priest self-propelled artillery fired point-blank at the Germans, stopping the enemy cold.

When the skies cleared, American Republic P-47 Thunderbolt fighter bombers of the XIX Tactical Air Command exacted a toll on the German tanks that were exposed in daylight while the American armor continued to hit targets of opportunity. The

coordination of American ground and air assets was superb, and after a week of fighting the Fifth Panzer Army was reduced to only twenty-five operational Panthers. By the time the Battle of Arracourt ended, the Germans had lost nearly ninety tanks while more than a hundred were disabled or experienced mechanical breakdowns. The 4th Armored Division lost forty-one Sherman tanks and seven M5 Stuart light tanks.

On December 16, 1944, the Germans launched Operation Wacht am Rhein (Watch on the Rhine). Hitler's last desperate gamble in the West resulted in the Battle of the Bulge, which ended in catastrophic defeat for the German army. Hitler had marshaled nearly thirty divisions, nine of them armored, and scores of his best Tiger and Panther tanks, hoping to breach the thinly held American line in the Ardennes Forest of France, Belgium, and Luxembourg. The

Above: An M4 Sherman tank accompanies US Marines across an open field on the island of Tinian in the Marianas. Control of three islands in the Marianas—Guam, Saipan, and Tinian—was critical to the prosecution of World War II against Japan. The Battle of Tinian took place the last week of July 1944. When the islands were secured, the Japanese home islands came within range of American heavy bombers. *US Marine Corps*

Left: As World War II in the Pacific progressed, the tactical concept of tank-infantry cooperation was refined. In this photo taken during the liberation of Guam in 1944, an M4 Sherman tank blasts a Japanese dugout with its 75mm main weapon. The supporting Marine riflemen stand ready to cut down any enemy troops who fled the smoldering structure. *US Marine Corps*

This composite hull Sherman is based on images of a US Army tank photographed on the Philippine island of Luzon in March 1944. Like their fellow servicemen in the sky, tankers sometimes adorned their machines with painted artwork.
Slawomir Zajaczkowski

German objective was the capture of the port of Antwerp, Belgium, a vital deepwater logistical hub for Allied operations. With Antwerp in German hands, British and American forces would be split, and supply efforts would grind to a virtual halt.

The sudden German onslaught surprised the Americans in the Ardennes, and initial progress was rapid. However, isolated pockets of resistance slowed the German spearheads. Intrepid combat engineers destroyed vital bridges to upset the enemy timetable. While the 7th Armored Division stubbornly defended St. Vith, tired paratroopers of the 101st Airborne along with Combat Command B of the 10th Armored Division grimly held onto another tactically critical Belgian crossroads town at Bastogne. Surrounded, the Americans in Bastogne forced the Germans to bypass the town to reach roads leading westward.

The powerful German tanks inflicted heavy casualties on American armored units, and young Cpl. Chuck Miller, a gunner aboard a Sherman tank with E Company, 32nd Armored Regiment, 3rd Armored Division, was lucky to escape with his life. One morning in early January, Miller's unit encountered German armor near the village of Sart, Belgium.

"... I was firing the 75mm gun at a German tank next to a barn. I had fired one armor piercing round when all of a sudden we received a direct hit to the turret," Miller recalled. "The shell hit the cupola ring and a flash of fire hit my periscope. The shell blew the tank commander's hatch open, took part of his head

off, and then proceeded to blow off the antiaircraft gun and mount. Bill Hey [the tank commander] was killed instantly and he fell down on my back, covering me with blood. . . . All I could think about was getting out of the tank, since when they hit you once they generally keep hitting you until the tank catches fire. . . ."

The deepest German penetration during the Battle of the Bulge occurred when tanks approached the River Meuse at Dinant, Belgium. Fifty miles distant from the German start line, Dinant was the high water mark of their advance. Counterattacks against the shoulders of the great bulge reduced the salient by the end of January 1945, and after six weeks of hard fighting the Germans had lost more than six hundred tanks and armored vehicles that could not be replaced.

One of the most heroic aspects of the Battle of the Bulge was the relief of Bastogne. Informed that

Left: African American soldiers of the 24th Infantry Regiment attached to the Americal Division of the US Army hug the ground at Empress Augusta Bay on the island of Bougainville during American operations against Japanese forces, which took place throughout most of 1944. The M4 Sherman tank accompanying the troops was superior to any armored vehicle fielded by the Japanese Army during World War II in the Pacific. *National Archives*

Below: Ninety minutes after the landing of the 3rd Marine Division on the island of Guam on July 21, 1944, the American beachhead is a beehive of activity. An M4 Sherman sits at the water's edge, its crew awaiting instructions to push ahead as Marines assault the island's well-entrenched Japanese defenders. *US Marine Corps*

An M4 advances up a dirt road on the island of Guam while riflemen of the 3rd Marine Division crouch warily to avoid Japanese snipers during the three-week battle to wrest control of the island from the enemy in July-August 1944. Guam is the largest of the Marianas islands, and its liberation was made more significant by the fact that it was American territory prior to its seizure by the Japanese in 1941. *US Marine Corps*

the situation was desperate there, General Patton, commanding the Third US Army, directed the bulk of his forces to disengage from an offensive in the Saar and pivot ninety degrees to the north to relieve the beleaguered defenders. Patton issued orders for the northward move on December 20. Battling winter weather and determined German resistance, the spearhead of the 4th Armored Division reached Bastogne on the day after Christmas.

The relief of Bastogne was arguably the finest hour for the Sherman and its soldiers during World War II in Europe. Major Albin Irzyk occupied the lead Sherman of the Eighth Tank Battalion, which led Combat Command B, which in turn was the vanguard of the 4th Armored Division. Irzyk was literally "up front for Patton" as he described the experience in

his memoirs years later. He remembered glancing to his rear and observing a seemingly endless strand of headlights, more Sherman tanks following at a purposeful pace.

Even while the Allies fought their way into Germany in the spring of 1945, the controversy surrounding the Sherman's combat capabilities continued to escalate. On March 19, nearly three months after the Battle of the Bulge, General Eisenhower wrote identical letters to Generals Maurice Rose and Isaac White, commanders of the 3rd and 2nd Armored Divisions respectively, asking their personal perspectives regarding the Sherman along with those of a representative number of tank commanders and soldiers. Surprisingly, Eisenhower displayed only a peripheral understanding of the situation.

Eisenhower's letter read in part, "Our men, in general, realize that the Sherman is not capable of standing up in a ding-dong, head-on fight with a Panther. Neither in gun power nor in armor is the present Sherman justified in undertaking such a contest. On the other hand, most of them realize that we have got a job of shipping tanks overseas and therefore do not want unwieldy monsters; that our tank has great reliability, good mobility, and that the gun in it has been vastly improved. . . ."

Rose responded, "It is my personal conviction that the present M4 and M4A3 tank is inferior to the German Mark V. . . . The fact that the M4 and M4A3 is inferior to the Mark V is borne out by the excessive number of losses we took while fighting in Belgium in December and January. The question naturally arises as to how I can account for the fact that in all of our operations against German armor we have been

successful if the statements I have heretofore made are to be accepted. The answer is that we compensate for our inferior equipment by the efficient use of artillery, air support, and maneuver, and in final analysis a great step toward equalizing our equipment is taken by the individual tanker and gunner, who maneuvers his tank and holds his fire until he is in position most favorable for him."

For those tankers and gunners who carried the fight to the Germans, survival was the top priority. One of the responses from the ranks came from Staff Sgt. Harry W. Wiggins, F Company, 33rd Armored Regiment, who noted, "I have fired at 150 yards at a Panther (six rounds—four APs and two HEs) without a penetration. This of course was at the front of a Panther, with a 75mm. We manage to get within effective range of German tanks because they are generally hiding or camouflaged and we try to engage them within a couple of hundred yards."

Staff Sergeant William G. Wilson of G Company, 33rd Armored Regiment, said succinctly, "The Mark V is way out ahead of our M4 in thickness and design of armor, and its gun. I think we have more speed and mobility than the Panther. I have seen M4s knock Panthers out at ranges under 800 yards (firing at the side of the enemy tanks), but it took a lot of nerve to stand there and pump out many rounds before getting a definite penetration."

It was inevitable that the debate over the Sherman would leak into the media, and while Eisenhower was asking for information from frontline tankers, General Patton defended the Sherman during press conferences, hoping to end "the foolish criticism" that was potentially undermining the fighting spirit of Allied soldiers.

Newspapers across the United States printed the text of a letter from Patton to Gen. Thomas T. Handy, deputy army chief of staff, praising the Sherman. ". . . It has been stated at home that these tanks are not comparable with the German Mark VI, the so-called Panther and Tiger type tanks. This statement is wholly incorrect for several reasons.

"Since Aug 1, 1944, when the 3rd army became operational, our total tank casualties have amounted

Negotiating a narrow jungle trail on the island of Bougainville in the Pacific in late 1944, a platoon of M4 Sherman tanks advances toward the front lines in support of US Marines. The M4 Sherman was more than a match for the lightly armed and armored Japanese tanks that were encountered from time to time during the Pacific War. Capable of destroying heavy Japanese fortifications, its 75mm gun provided additional firepower. *Voyageur Press collection*

After firing on a Japanese pillbox on the island of Guam in the Marianas, an M4 Sherman tank idles as the Marine riflemen accompanying it prepare to fire on Japanese soldiers attempting to exit the concrete-reinforced position. *US Marine Corps*

to 1,136 tanks. During the same period we have accounted for 2,287 German tanks, of which 808 were of the Tiger or Panther variety, and 851 on our side were M-4. . . . It is patent that if a Tiger tank with an enormous thickness of armor were put at one end of a village street and engaged in a fire fight with a M-4 tank at the other end, the M-4 tank would not last. However, the great mobility of the M-4 usually enables it to circumvent the slow and unwieldy Tigers and not to engage in a slugging match but to attack them from the rear."

For those doing the fighting, killing, and dying, the experience at war with the Sherman was often more than excruciating. Belton Y. Cooper served as a lieutenant with the 3rd Armored Division. Decades later, he authored the book *Death Traps: The Survival of an American Armored Division in World War II*. The 1998 volume tells a harrowing tale of death and destruction.

Although *Death Traps* is controversial, Cooper said of the 3rd Armored Division's experience in World War II,

"We lost 648 medium tanks. We had another 700 repaired and put back into action. When you compare that to the original 232 we had when we landed at Normandy, I don't know of any other division or service that took that kind of loss."

Cooper calculated the 3rd Armored Division's loss rate in tanks at 580 percent. The classic conundrum in balancing armor protection, firepower, and mobility, particularly as it relates to the M4 Sherman in Western Europe during World War II, remains a prominent topic of historical debate.

Meanwhile, in the Pacific no such debate existed. The Japanese armed forces devoted little in the way of resources to the development of tanks. The Type 95 Ha-Go light tank and the Type 97 Chi-Ha medium tank were lightly armored and mounted 37mm and 57mm main weapons respectively. With the outbreak of World War II, the M3 Stuart light tank outclassed the Type 95, while the M4 Sherman was

Above: A US Marine rifleman takes aim at a distant target while another crouches to present a low profile to Japanese snipers on Okinawa. Meanwhile, a flamethrowing M4 Sherman tank spews fire at a hardened enemy gun emplacement. The Japanese usually fought to the death, and Marines were forced to use flamethrowers and demolition charges to subdue them. *US Marine Corps*

Opposite: A flamethrowing M4 Sherman tank leads the way for Marines advancing through the rugged terrain of Okinawa. The M4 provided valuable service during the conquest of the island in the spring of 1945. However, it was vulnerable to Japanese mines, antitank weapons, and suicide squads that would deliberately carry explosives beneath the tanks and detonate them. *US Marine Corps*

vastly superior in firepower and armor protection to anything the Japanese fielded.

Tank versus tank engagements were rare in the Pacific Theater; however, the availability of American armor was often critical to the success of offensive operations during the Allied march across the Pacific toward the home islands of Japan. Sherman tanks blasted machine gun nests, blockhouses, and bunkers that the Japanese had constructed of reinforced concrete, coconut logs, and heaps of sand. The M4A3 R3 flamethrower variant of the Sherman served with US Marines at Iwo Jima and Okinawa, spewing jets of flaming gasoline into the mouths of caves or the gun apertures of bunkers to burn or suffocate enemy inhabitants.

During the battle for control of the islet of Betio at Tarawa Atoll in the Gilbert Islands in November

1943, accompanying armor struggled to get ashore in support of the hard-fighting 2nd Marine Division. Shermans fell into deep holes off the beaches and were lost. Two were accidentally destroyed by American dive bombers, and others were committed to the battle piecemeal without specific orders.

Late on November 20, the first day of fighting, only two Shermans remained in action. On Red Beach 3, Colorado, under the command of Lt. Louis Largey, supported a Marine drive toward an airstrip. Japanese antitank guns zeroed in on the Sherman, but the tank continued to advance, even undeterred when it set off a mine. Colorado's 75mm gun belched, and its machine gun barrels heated up with continuous fire. On Green Beach, Lt. Ed Bale commanded a Sherman named China Gal, which destroyed a Japanese tank after taking a hit from its 37mm gun that failed to penetrate the Sherman's armor but turned the inside of its turret lemon yellow.

After taking serious punishment, the blackened hulk of China Gal continued rumbling along, supporting the marines on Green Beach. On the second day of the battle, another Sherman, nicknamed Cecilia, had been repaired and joined China Gal to lead the Leathernecks across Betio. The barren landscape in front of the tanks became a killing ground, and the marines killed 250 Japanese defenders in less than three hours.

As the end approached, marines took on the concrete bunker of the Japanese commander, Adm. Keiji Shibasaki. Colorado fired a 75mm round that cracked open the structure, but stubborn Japanese defenders continued to fire. Marine engineers stormed the bunker with satchel charges, and when these detonated enemy troops poured into the open. Colorado killed twenty of them with a single canister round. The Japanese had believed the island fortress of Betio was unconquerable, but with the help of the Shermans, the marines took their objective in four grueling days of savage fighting.

When the US Army's 754th Tank Battalion on the island of New Caledonia received its new Sherman tanks in January 1944, Col. Gino Amorelli called the event a "big morale booster." The battalion later fought in the jungles of Bougainville and the Philippines. Supporting the 129th Infantry Regiment of the 37th Division on Bougainville in March 1944, the tanks of the 754th Regiment fought off a Japanese attack and continuously engaged the enemy for three weeks. In one engagement, a platoon of Sherman tanks from C Company counterattacked along with infantry as the Japanese took cover in several small ravines. The cooperating tanks and troops silenced two pillboxes.

The attack was suspended to replenish ammunition, and a fresh platoon of tanks came up to silence the remaining Japanese pillboxes. A third tank platoon then arrived, and three Shermans led the renewed advance with a pair of M3 Stuart light tanks covering their flanks. Along with their attached

infantry, the American tanks attacked in waves, firing canister at the Japanese. As the fighting waned, one Sherman was damaged and more than a hundred enemy troops were killed in an afternoon.

By the end of World War II, the M4 Sherman medium tank had undoubtedly contributed to the Allied victory on all fronts. Its reputation for reliability and speed had been well earned. Nevertheless, the Sherman had also been the subject of harsh criticism. It is worthy of note, however, that much of the criticism leveled at the tank itself emanated from the employment of the prevailing tank doctrine as it was tested on the battlefield in real time.

Below: Riflemen of Col. Victor Bleasdale's 29th Marine Regiment hitch a ride aboard an M4 Sherman tank, which raises a cloud of dust as it speeds along a dirt road in Okinawa. As this photo was taken, the Marines were racing to occupy the town of Ghuta ahead of the Japanese. *US Marine Corps*

Opposite: A US Marine M4 rolls down a dirt road in the Okinawan village of Naha as two Marine riflemen follow along. The bitter fighting for Okinawa, costly though it was, would have exacted a much higher toll in American blood without the contribution of Marine armor. *US Marine Corps*

PART IV
REMARKABLE LONGEVITY

CHAPTER SEVEN

Extended Service Life

In the wake of World War II, the M4 Sherman tank—in all its various configurations, adaptations, and derivatives—remained one of the most recognizable and available weapons systems across the globe.

No other weapon of its kind had been produced in such great numbers by a Western power or distributed across such a spectrum of combat theaters. The harnessing of the American automobile industry in wartime had made both the finished tank and the spare parts needed to keep it running available in abundance. Even though practical combat experience had fueled debate as to its performance and contributed to the rise of the concept of the "main battle tank," which would come to dominate the modern battlefield by the end of the twentieth century, the Sherman was reliable, adaptable, and most of all, available. After World War II, the opportunities for its continuing deployment were hardly diminished.

The exodus of the Allied powers from former operations areas, the rise of the Third World, and the emergence of the Cold War fostered continuing tensions and distrust among the former military partners that had defeated the Axis. Additionally, the tinderbox of the Middle East erupted in warfare with the birth of the state of Israel, while the divided Korean Peninsula was the scene of a brutal ideologically driven clash. So, too, the separation of Vietnam into Communist North and Democratic South resulted in open warfare, while the Indian subcontinent was torn by territorial and religious disputes.

United Nations infantrymen follow directly behind an M4 Sherman tank while probing North Korean positions on the outskirts of Seoul, the South Korean capital. The Korean War began when the communist North Koreans invaded South Korea on June 25, 1950. *US Army*

The Sherman remained a frontline tank for some time and then became a common reserve weapon as a new generation of armored fighting vehicles was developed. From the tank's first deployment during World War II into the 1990s, the armed forces of more than fifty nations fielded some variant of the M4 Sherman.

With the outbreak of the Korean War on June 25, 1950, North Korean forces crossed the 38th Parallel and invaded South Korea. The North Koreans deployed the Soviet-built T-34 medium tank of World War II fame; initially, the heaviest South Korean and American tanks available to fight under the United Nations flag were M24 Chaffees hurriedly shipped from Japan, mounting a 75mm gun but lightly armored and incapable of standing up to the T-34. The US Army had approximately 3,400 M4A3E8 Shermans—the "Easy Eight" of World War II vintage—in its inventory. Although only about half

of these were operational, a substantial number were deployed with UN forces, including the South Korean Army. The heavier M26 Pershing and M46 Patton tanks were introduced during the course of the war.

The Sherman remained at a disadvantage in tank-versus-tank combat with the T-34 but continued to excel in an infantry support role. On March 7, 1951, Shermans of Company A, 89th Medium Tank Battalion crossed the Han River in support of the 35th Infantry Regiment, 25th Division. As the infantrymen crossed the river in small boats, they came under small-arms fire. The tanks began fording the river in darkness and concentrated their early fire on a hilltop, silencing Chinese machine guns.

A pair of Shermans continued toward a line of six burned-out railroad cars and attacked three enemy machine gun emplacements positioned to fire to the south, underneath the cars. The tanks raked the Chinese with their .30-caliber hull-mounted machine

Top left: This "white" Sherman has been modified to transport scientists near the blast site of the 1945 atomic bomb test at Alamogordo, New Mexico. The turret has been replaced with an enclosed cupola, and most of the tank's hatches have been sealed to guard against radiation. *Voyageur Press collection*

Top right: The M4 Sherman tank's service life spanned well over half a century with the armed forces of nations around the world. In this photo, four members of an Argentine Army M4 crew pose in front of their Sherman in 1950. *Voyageur Press collection*

Opposite: Medics carry a litter bearing a wounded soldier of the US 24th Infantry Division In Korea, while an M4 Sherman tank covers the evacuation with its 76mm main weapon and .30- and .50-caliber machine guns. The crew of the M4 has nicknamed the armored vehicle "Leilani." The Sherman remained a frontline tank for some time after World War II before becoming a common reserve weapon as a new generation of armored fighting vehicles was developed. *Voyageur Press collection*

guns and then fired up to fifteen rounds from their 76mm weapons, destroying the positions. Rolling forward, the Americans encountered three more enemy machine gun nests, and Lt. Thomas Allie, leading the 3rd Platoon, ordered his gunner to fire two 76mm rounds at the new target. The second round blew weapons, equipment, and the body parts of enemy soldiers into the air.

Allie's platoon of four Shermans then stood side by side to lay down withering machine gun fire against the Chinese. The accompanying infantrymen of the 35th Regiment advanced another seven hundred yards to

assault and capture their objective under the protective cover of the tanks.

Tankers of the US Marines' Company A, 1st Tank Battalion, were ordered to Korea with the 1st Provisional Marine Brigade. They had trained in the M4A3 and had little time to transition to the M26. The heavy tanks and a contingent of M4A3 dozer tanks participated in the defense of the Pusan Perimeter in late 1950 and the subsequent actions at the Chosin Reservoir. A single M4A3 Sherman led the successful marine breakout from the "Frozen Chosin" in December of that year.

Castro Takes a Ride

In February 1957, the Cuban government of Fulgencio Batista received seven American M4 Sherman medium tanks. Two years later, the island nation was battling Marxist revolutionaries led by Fidel Castro, and the Cuban military utilized these armored vehicles in their fight against the insurgency.

During the decisive battle for control of the city of Santa Clara, the revolutionaries under the command of Castro's lieutenant, Che Guevara, captured several Sherman tanks intact and effectively completed the defeat of Batista's forces. One famous photograph depicts Che in front of an M4A3(76)W, his left arm in a sling, barking orders to a soldier.

On January 8, 1959, just a few days after the victory at Santa Clara, Castro triumphantly entered the Cuban capital city of Havana. An observer reported later, ". . . Fidel Castro, with his ten-year-old son, Fidelito, on one side and one of his most trusted guerrilla fighters, Major Huber Matos, on the other, rolled into Havana on a US-made Sherman tank. At least one million Cubans lined the highway and streets, shouting and yelling, 'Gracias, Fidel!'"

Later that year and with US support, Cuban opponents of Castro came ashore at the Bay of Pigs, intent on toppling the Marxist regime. Castro's Sherman tanks were there to oppose the landings.

En route from the mountains of the Sierra Maestra to the Cuban capital city of Havana, young victorious revolutionary Fidel Castro carries an armload of newspapers as he passes an M4 Sherman medium tank. The M4 was involved in the Marxist revolution that brought Castro to power on January 1, 1959. *Lee Lockwood/Getty Images*

In this photo taken on January 4, 1951, an American M4 Sherman tank crosses the Han River during the evacuation of the South Korean capital of Seoul before the onslaught of North Korean forces. The pontoon bridge spanning the waterway was destroyed shortly after the tank completed its crossing. *US Army*

During the autumn of 1951 at the Battle of Heartbreak Ridge, M4A3E8s of the US Army's 72nd Tank Battalion were heavily engaged with Chinese infantry, antitank guns, and mines. The tanks destroyed scores of Chinese weapons and raked enemy troop concentrations with their machine guns and 76mm cannon, providing UN forces the necessary firepower to eventually secure the ridge. However, the tanks lost heavily during a month of fighting, with thirty-eight Shermans destroyed and nine damaged.

The M4 Sherman was also associated with the conflict in Vietnam throughout French efforts to suppress the Viet Minh insurgency in the early 1950s and on a limited basis during the US involvement in Southeast Asia that began a decade later. A relative few M4s also served with the South Vietnamese Army; however, armored engagements were rare during the Vietnam War and American tanks of the Patton series bore the brunt of combat.

During the years immediately after World War II, the governments of the United States, Great Britain, and France sought to exert some control over postwar arms proliferation, particularly in Palestine and other hotspots around the globe. The three nations formed

a cooperative venture known as the Near East Arms Coordinating Committee, and though the initiative soon ended with mixed results due in part to Soviet arms sales around the world, the committee nevertheless monitored the distribution of military hardware. In October 1952, it estimated that the Syrian army had fielded at least fifty-two Sherman tanks. It was also known that elements of the Indian army had fought with British forces during World War II and retained their Sherman V tanks, many of which had seen action against the Japanese in Burma.

When the nation of Israel came into being in the spring of 1948, its existence was immediately threatened. The armed forces of neighboring Arab nations invaded and a fight for the survival of the new Jewish state ensued. Poorly armed and equipped, the Haganah, forerunner of the Israeli Defense Forces (IDF), obtained a handful of Sherman tanks, some of them from British soldiers who had been ordered to render them inoperative but instead allowed the fighters to take them. The Israelis also reportedly obtained approximately thirty more Shermans in various states of disrepair from an Italian junkyard. At the end of the war for independence, it is estimated that only fourteen Israeli Sherman tanks remained operational.

Although embargoes of arms sales to Israel occurred regularly during the coming years, the IDF did receive clandestine arms shipments. For a time, France supplied modern weapons to Israel on a covert basis and with US support. The United States also provided modern tanks of the Patton series to the Israelis. However, with significant modifications, the Sherman was a mainstay of the Israeli armored forces for some time, destined to serve in combat with the IDF during four major wars from 1948 through 1973.

Israeli engineers accomplished several modifications to the existing Sherman configurations and produced powerful innovations that were designated the M-50 and M-51, both popularly known as the "Super Sherman." Among the earliest concerns for the IDF was the development of a tank that could counter the battle-tested Soviet-supplied T-34 medium and IS-3 heavy tanks of the Egyptian army. The immediate solution lay in the upgunning of existing Shermans, a feat accomplished with the assistance of the French government.

By the early 1950s, France had become a major arms-exporting nation, and a delegation of Israeli army and government officials visited the country to observe trials of the new AMX-13 light tank. The main armament of the AMX-13 was the high-velocity 75mm CN 75-50 cannon, patterned after the well-known German 75mm KwK 42 L70 cannon that had been mounted on the formidable PzKpfw. V Panther medium tank during World War II.

Opposite: Painted with the image of a ferocious tiger, this M4 and its crew pose for a photograph along the banks of the Han River near Seoul, South Korea, in 1951. American and South Korean armored units sometimes emblazoned their tanks with such images since the Chinese were believed to be deathly afraid of the tiger. *Department of Defense*

Right: On October 14, 1951, soldiers of a demolition squad of Company A, 65th Engineer Battalion, 25th Infantry Division, place explosives under the tracks of a disabled M4 to prevent it from being recovered by the advancing North Koreans. Soldiers of the recovery platoon of Company C, 89th Tank Battalion, 25th Infantry Division, watch the engineers work. *US Army*

Below: A poster promoting the 1958 movie *Tank Battalion* features a stylized M4 taking the measure of communist troops who flee in terror before them. *Voyageur Press collection*

While they purchased the AMX-13, the Israelis also recognized an opportunity to improve the battlefield prowess of their Sherman tanks. In 1954, a program was undertaken to marry the M4 Sherman chassis with the high-velocity French gun. The result was the M-50, and the first twenty-five of these upgunned Shermans reached the IDF in 1956, just prior to Operation Kadesh, also known as the Suez Crisis, the unsuccessful joint operation with Israeli, British, and French forces invading Egypt to gain control of the Suez Canal, curb terrorist activities, and possibly topple Egyptian President Gamal Abdel Nasser.

The M-50 turret was modified with a prominent counterweight to stabilize the heavier gun, and early conversions proved too heavy for the original engine, the old Continental R-975, while the vertical volute spring suspension was inadequate for cross-country performance with the additional weight. Subsequent

Clearing a road somewhere in South Korea on February 6, 1952, an M4 tank dozer of the US Army's 9th Tank Company, 9th Regiment, 2nd Infantry Division, demonstrates the versatility of the M4 tank's armored chassis. The chassis served as the platform for a variety of combat and service vehicles. *US Army*

A US Army M4A3R3 Sherman tank, equipped with a flamethrower, spews fire at a target during maneuvers somewhere in Korea. This photo was taken in 1953, while peace negotiations to end the Korean War were ongoing. The flamethrower tank was often the ideal means of neutralizing enemy strongpoints that were otherwise virtually impervious to direct assault. *Voyageur Press collection*

conversions to the M-50 were powered by the Cummins V-8 diesel engine and reequipped with the improved horizontal volute spring suspension.

At the time of the Suez Crisis, the IDF fielded approximately two hundred World War II–era Sherman tanks, some of which had not been modified to the M-50 standard. Conversions to the M-50 did continue into the 1960s, and approximately three hundred Shermans were eventually improved along with a quantity of M10 Wolverine tank destroyers that also utilized the M4 chassis. During the Six-Day War of 1967 and the Yom Kippur War of 1973, the M-50 remained active, fighting against other Shermans then in service with the Egyptian

army and a new generation of Soviet-built tanks that were flooding the world arms export market, the T-54/55 and the T-62.

The second major Israeli upgrade to the Sherman involved the existing stock of IDF M4A1 tanks along with the cooperation of French armor designers. The French 105mm CN 105 F1 cannon was thoroughly evaluated and proven to be one of the finest weapons of its kind available in the early 1960s. The main gun of the French AMX-30 tank, the 105mm F1, was shortened for use with the modified T-23 turret of the M4A1, and the powerful result was the M-51, also generally referred to as the "Super Sherman," but known in some quarters as the "Isherman" ("I" standing for improved). Again, the

Tanks often served as mobile artillery platforms during the Korean War, and this M4 Sherman fulfills that role as it lobs 76mm shells at North Korean positions across the Han River near the city of Seoul, the South Korean capital. *John Dominis/The LIFE Picture Collection/Getty Images*

ראשון לציון
29 לאפריל

תערוכת
הצבא
1957

Isherman incorporated the Cummins V-8 diesel engine and the horizontal volute spring suspension.

Eventually, 180 M4A1s were upgraded to the M-51 model. The tank was unveiled publicly during Israel's Independence Day observances in the spring of 1965. Perhaps the ultimate of the Sherman fighting tank designs, the M-51 arrived more than twenty years after the first M4 tanks rolled off American assembly lines.

During the Six-Day War, more than 2,500 tanks were deployed by the IDF and the opposing armies of Egypt, Jordan, Syria, and other Arab countries. The Israeli armor consisted of the M-50, M-51, AMX-13, and newer British Centurion tanks, while the Arab forces included the T-34/85, the Soviet-built medium tank of World War II fame upgunned with an 85mm cannon, the SU-100 tank destroyer, the T-54/55, and American-built M48 Pattons along with a few older M4 Shermans. Israeli tanks and tactics proved more than capable of defeating the Arab armor, including the T-54/55 and the M48.

On June 5 through 6, 1967, Israeli tanks and troops under the command of Generals Avraham Yoffe and Ariel Sharon, the future prime minister of Israel, were

Left: During the Six-Day War of 1967, the Israeli Defense Force utilized the upgunned and modernized Super Sherman tank based on the original World War II–era armored fighting vehicle. The Super Sherman in this image, taken on June 5, 1967, rests near the twisted remains of an unidentified armored vehicle that was destroyed in earlier fighting on the road between Bethlehem and Jerusalem. *Pierre Guillaud/AFP/Getty Images*

Bottom: An M4A1E6 Sherman tank of the Pakistani Army lies abandoned after it was destroyed in combat with Indian Army units during one of numerous border clashes between the two countries. Battle damage to the hull and turret indicates that the armor of the tank was penetrated three times. *Voyageur Press collection*

Opposite: Israeli soldiers advance along a dirt road in the Sinai desert during a salvage and cleanup operation during the Suez Crisis of 1956. One of the vehicles they are evaluating is a destroyed M4 Sherman tank that appears to have been hit multiple times. *David Rubinger/The LIFE Images Collection/Getty Images*

ordered to take the key crossroads town of Abu Ageila in the northern Sinai Peninsula. The Centurions of an independent tank battalion and two battalions of armored infantry along with two battalions of Super Shermans from the 14th Armored Brigade, a total of about one hundred tanks, took on the Egyptian 12th Brigade with sixty-six T-34/85s of the 6th Tank Regiment and a mechanized antitank battalion of twenty-two SU-100s.

In the ensuing melee, the Israelis attacked from several directions and knocked out forty Egyptian tanks and armored vehicles for the loss of nineteen Israeli

Opposite: The crew of an Indian M4 Sherman tank pauses for a photographer during a break in the fighting against Pakistani forces. During the Indo-Pakistani Wars of 1965 and 1971, both the Indian and Pakistani armies deployed the M4. *National Army Museum, London via Bridgeman Images*

Right: On June 5, 1967, Israel launched preemptive attacks against Egypt and Syria, resulting in a lightning victory for the Israeli Defense Force during the Six-Day War. This photo depicts two Israeli Super Sherman tanks on patrol in East Jerusalem on June 10. *Pierre Guillaud/Getty Images*

tanks, of which at least seven were Centurions. Israeli casualties amounted to 40 killed and 140 wounded, while the Egyptians suffered about 4,000 dead.

In the early hours of the 1973 Yom Kippur War, IDF tanks proved extremely vulnerable to Egyptian tank killer teams armed with the Soviet-made RPG-7 shoulder-fired rocket and the lethal 9K11 Malyutka antitank missile, identified in NATO nomenclature as the AT-3 Sagger. On October 6, the Egyptians achieved complete surprise, crossing the Suez Canal in rubber boats and small craft and piercing the thin Israeli defenses of the Bar-Lev Line with the support of eight hundred tanks that were ferried to the Israeli side aboard barges and crossed on pontoon bridges hastily thrown together by engineers. Only twenty Egyptian tanks were lost in the initial assault.

Simultaneously, the Syrian army struck to the north along the strategically vital Golan Heights. Three Syrian mechanized divisions—the 5th, 7th, and 9th—attacked Israeli positions with infantry supported by eight hundred tanks. The 176 tanks and supporting infantrymen of the Barak and 7th Armored Brigades of the IDF were all that stood between the Syrians and the Israeli capital city of Tel Aviv. At the end of the first day of fighting, the Barak Brigade was down to only fifteen serviceable tanks. Fierce fighting raged for several days on the heights and in the neighboring Valley of Tears.

Recovering from the initial shock of the Arab onslaught, the IDF responded against Egyptian and Syrian armor with the American-made wire-guided TOW antitank missile, taking a significant toll. The Israeli Armored Corps consisted of approximately three thousand tanks at the outbreak of the Yom Kippur War. Among these were the M48 and new M60 tanks of the American Patton series armed with 90mm and 105mm guns. The first of the advanced M60s had only recently arrived and deployed with the 401st Armored Brigade.

Earlier Patton tanks were modified to Israeli specifications and referred to as the Magach Series. Alongside them were the aging M-50 and M-51 Super Shermans and modified Centurions that the Israelis designated the Sho't. Some of the Super Shermans and Centurions had been upgraded to the new British 105mm L7 cannon.

The Israelis faced approximately 1,700 Egyptian tanks of varying capabilities organized in twenty-six armored brigades along with roughly 1,200 tanks of the Syrian army. Both Arab forces included the T-34/85, many of which had been in service since the late 1950s. However, the Egyptians and Syrians had received significant quantities of the newer Soviet-designed T-54/55 and T-62 tanks, with their 100mm and 115mm guns respectively, to replace their grievous losses suffered during the Six-Day War.

In an exchange with Iraqi tanks on October 12, 1973, the IDF 17th and 19th Brigades, including Super Shermans, destroyed eighty enemy armored vehicles at the village of Nasej near the Golan Heights. The 19th Brigade went on to engage Jordanian armor later in the month.

On October 14, a week after their opening foray, the Egyptians committed six armored brigades to the capture of high ground in the Sinai, initiating the largest armored battle since World War II. Eight hundred Israeli tanks opposed at least one thousand Egyptian tanks, and in the end the superior combined-arms tactics of the Israelis contributed to their victory. Utilizing company-sized formations, IDF tanks attacked while antitank missiles hissed toward the enemy from prepared positions and accurate artillery fire disrupted the coordination of the Egyptian tanks and troops.

When the single day of bitter combat was over, the Egyptians had suffered tremendous losses with 264 tanks totally destroyed or disabled. In exchange, the Israelis lost forty tanks. Assuming the offensive, the IDF rolled westward, crossing the Suez Canal and trapping the entire Egyptian Third Army. On the Golan Heights, the Sho't, Magach, and Super Sherman tanks destroyed up to one thousand Syrian tanks during a week of heavy fighting, seized the initiative, and then advanced to within thirty miles of the Syrian capital of Damascus.

During the Battle of the Chinese Farm on the 15th, the IDF 143rd Armored Division, under the command of General Sharon, lost 70 of its 250 tanks in a single night of combat. Even during their retreat, the Egyptian infantry deftly handled its Sagger antitank missiles. One tank-killing squad of the 19th Infantry Division destroyed or disabled nine Israeli tanks, expending all its Saggers in the process.

At the end of the brief but bloody Yom Kippur War, the IDF had recovered and won a significant victory. However, the cost had been high. At least one thousand tanks had been lost, and the Israeli military establishment had been shaken to its core. The performance of the Israeli tanks had contributed mightily to the eventual rout of the Arab forces, and readily apparent among its achievements was the validation of the programs that not only introduced modern tanks to the IDF organization but also continually upgraded the venerable M4 Sherman tank. The Super Shermans, though fast approaching obsolescence, had held their own against a new generation of Soviet-made tanks. It was a remarkable achievement that occurred thirty years after the Sherman's combat debut at El Alamein in 1943.

Opposite: With the bodies of dead enemy soldiers lying before them, Indian troops pause on either side of a captured Pakistani M4 Sherman medium tank following a battle during the Indo-Pakistani War of 1965. The armed forces of both India and Pakistan fielded the M4 during their conflicts of the 1960s and 70s. *Rolls Press/Popperfoto/ Getty Images*

The Israeli Defense Force carried innovation to another level with the chassis of the M4 Sherman tank. During its long service with the IDF, the M4 was modified not only as a capable combat tank but also as an assault gun, fire-support howitzer, rocket launcher platform, and recovery vehicle.

During the Suez Crisis and the Six-Day War, both Arab and Israeli forces deployed the towed French 155mm Howitzer Model 1950. The Israelis developed the self-propelled M-50 assault gun, mounting the 155mm howitzer atop the chassis of the M4 tank. By 1968, the Soltam Systems M68 L33 155mm self-propelled Howitzer was in service with the IDF's 188th Armoured Brigade, combining the 155mm L33 gun-howitzer developed by the Israeli

firm with the chassis of the now-legendary M4A3E8 Easy Eight Sherman.

The M4 chassis remained in use with the IDF into the 1980s, and one of its latest modifications was the MAR-290, mounting four 290mm rocket-firing tubes. The MAR-290, also known as the Episkopi, was an improvement of an Israeli-built copy of the highly successful Soviet BM-24 multiple launch rocket system, which entered service during the Israeli invasion of Lebanon in 1982.

Altogether, Israeli designers produced at least a dozen Sherman tank variants during the service life of the chassis that spanned five decades. Among other innovations were the Makmat 160mm, developed in 1968 with an open-topped M4 chassis

Above: As a formation of Israeli Super Sherman tanks takes up positions encircling the old town of Jerusalem from the north during the Six-Day War of 1967, a Super Sherman halts at the foot of Mount Scopus with the Hebrew University in the background. *Ullstein Bild/Getty Images*

Opposite: An Israeli Super Sherman tank kicks up a cloud of desert dust as it advances against enemy forces during the Yom Kippur War on October 13, 1973. The Israelis modified the older M4 Sherman medium tank to produce the M-50 and M-51 versions of the Super Sherman. *Keystone-France/Getty Images*

mounting the Soltam M-66 160mm mortar and serving into the late 1980s; the MAR-240 rocket launcher with thirty-six 240mm rocket tubes; the Kilshon anti-radiation missile system that mounted the AGM-45 Shrike missile atop an open-turreted M4 chassis; the Sherman Medical Evacuation Tank, modified with the engine forward and space in the rear of the hull to carry four combat casualties; the Trailblazer recovery vehicle with a single-boom crane atop the M4A1 chassis; and the Eyal observation post vehicle, which carried a hydraulic ninety-foot observation platform.

The partition of India in 1947 led to territorial disputes and to major wars between India and Pakistan in 1965 and 1971. Both nations deployed armor extensively, and the M4 Sherman played a prominent role in each conflict.

When the nations went to war in 1965, the Pakistani army included more than two thousand tanks in fifteen armored cavalry regiments, each of them organized into three squadrons of approximately forty-five tanks. These included the M47 and M48 Patton, the M24 Chaffee, and about two hundred M4 Shermans. In the early 1950s, the US government approved the sale of two hundred Sherman tanks to the Indian army, and later in the decade the Indians had begun modernizing their armored contingent with the addition of 164 French AMX-13 tanks and 188 British Centurions, and its 2nd Armored Brigade was fully equipped with Centurions. However, within its single armored division, the 1st "Black Elephant" Division, and seventeen cavalry regiments, the majority were Shermans and light M3A3 Stuart tanks.

During the Yom Kippur War of 1973, an Israeli M32 armored recovery vehicle tows a Super Sherman tank, originally manufactured in the United States and heavily modified by the Israelis, which has apparently been disabled in action or broken down. The M32 was one of many specially purposed vehicles that utilized the chassis of the M4 Sherman medium tank. *Rolls Press/Popperfoto/Getty Images*

In this 1983 photo, US Marines run past the rusting hulk of a World War II–era M4 Sherman tank during physical training. Relics of a bygone period of extreme violence, numerous examples of M4 Sherman tanks remain accessible around the world. Some of these have been dedicated as monuments, while others lie abandoned and derelict. *Department of Defense*

Most of the Indian Shermans were the M4A1 improved with the 76mm main weapon during World War II, while others had been more recently modified with the 75mm French CN 75-50 cannon after the Israeli example. The Pakistani Shermans included M4A2s that had seen action during the Korean War and were then provided to Pakistan's military in 1954 through the Mutual Defense Assistance Program, the first US military aid program formalized during the Cold War.

During three days of fighting from September 8 to 10, 1965, Pakistani tanks, although marginally superior from a technological standpoint, suffered severe losses. Elements of the Pakistani 1st Armored Division, the army's premier tank force—including the 19th Lancers, 12th Cavalry, 24th Cavalry, 4th Cavalry, 5th

Horse, and 6th Lancers—stumbled into an Indian trap at Asal Uttar in the state of Punjab.

Three Indian armored regiments—the 3rd Cavalry, Deccan Horse, and 8th Cavalry—took up defensive positions in the shape of a U, allowing the Pakistani armor to advance into a three-sided attack. While the Indian tanks were concealed among tall sugarcane stalks, the Pakistanis failed to send out reconnaissance elements and came under heavy artillery bombardment.

The Indians waited until their enemy was at point-blank range and then opened up with their 75mm, 76mm, and 90mm guns, destroying or disabling nearly one hundred Pakistani tanks. Scores of others were abandoned on the field.

Concurrent with the action at Asal Uttar, a series of large tank engagements collectively known as the Battle of Chawinda took place from September 6 to 22. This time, the Indian Black Elephant Division was pounded, losing at least 120 tanks. A number of these were venerable Shermans that fell to the high-velocity guns of modern Pakistani tanks. Pakistani losses at Chawinda amounted to about forty tanks.

During thirteen days of fighting in December 1971, the Indian army compelled Pakistani forces to withdraw from East Pakistan and assisted in the establishment of the government of Bangladesh. The Pakistanis suffered from flawed tactics. Their M47 and M48 Pattons were superior in armor protection and firepower to the Soviet-supplied PT-76 amphibious tanks and AMX-13s of the Indians. However, these advantages were negated when Pakistani commanders deployed their heavier tanks in small troops of only two or three each rather than large formations.

The Pakistanis also deployed an ever-decreasing number of venerable M24 Chaffee and M4 Sherman tanks, and on rare occasions their worn 75mm and 76mm guns proved themselves still potent when a thinly armored Indian PT-76 or AMX-13 ventured into the open.

During a long service career that began seventy-five years ago, the Sherman tank has literally gone global. In addition to the Allied powers that won World War II and the countries that faced one another on the battlefields of the Middle East, the Indian subcontinent, and the Korean Peninsula, the Sherman found its way to Asia and South America.

The tank saw service with both Communist and Nationalist forces during the Chinese Civil War of the late 1940s and equipped the reconstituted Japanese Self-Defense Force and the Philippine army into the 1960s. During the same period, Argentina purchased 450 Sherman tanks, many of them British Firefly variants, from Belgium. These tanks were modernized in the 1970s during the Argentine border crisis with neighboring Chile.

Meanwhile, Chile had purchased one hundred of Israel's aged Super Shermans in the late 1970s,

and these remained in service until the 1990s, when they were retired in favor of reconditioned German-designed Leopard 1V tanks sold to the Chileans by the government of the Netherlands and by the French AMX-30B2. The Chilean Super Shermans may in fact have been the last combat tanks of M4 lineage in service.

The armed forces of France, Denmark, Portugal, the Netherlands, Yugoslavia, Italy, and Greece are among the European countries that utilized some variant of the Sherman, either a combat tank, artillery platform, or recovery vehicle, into the 1970s. Mexico operated the M32 Chenca armored recovery vehicle as recently as 1998.

The last Sherman tanks to see combat may well have been M4A3s in service with the Nicaraguan National Guard during the Sandinista Revolution of 1978–1979. Considering the long service life of the M4 Sherman, however, it is possible that somewhere in the world the old workhorse remains active even today.

Above: Israeli-backed militiamen of the South Lebanese Army patrol near the town of Tibnin in company with a venerable Sherman tank that was more than forty years old when these photos were taken in the spring of 1987. The Israelis upgraded Sherman tanks in numerous ways and extended their service lives considerably. The tank retains a degraded camouflage scheme that has faded to a dull gray. *David Rubinger/ The LIFE Images Collection/Getty Images*

Opposite: Built in 1943, this M4 Sherman tank has been conserved as a monument to the men and the machines that contributed so much to victory in World War II. Numerous M4s are on display as memorials and tributes around the world. *DEA/G. Cigolini/Getty Images*

INDEX

Page numbers in italics indicate an illustration or caption.

© 2016 Quarto Publishing Group USA Inc.
Text © 2016 Michael E. Haskew

First published in 2016 by Voyageur Press, an imprint of Quarto Publishing Group USA Inc.,
400 First Avenue North, Suite 400, Minneapolis, MN 55401 USA.
Telephone: (612) 344-8100 Fax: (612) 344-8692

quartoknows.com
Visit our blogs at quartoknows.com

Voyageur Press titles are also available at discounts in bulk quantity for industrial or sales-promotional use.
For details contact the Special Sales Manager at Quarto Publishing Group USA Inc., 400 First Avenue North,
Suite 400, Minneapolis, MN 55401 USA.

10 9 8 7 6 5 4 3 2 1

ISBN: 978-0-7603-5030-0

Library of Congress Cataloging-in-Publication Data

Names: Haskew, Michael E., author.
Title: M4 Sherman tanks : the illustrated history of America's most iconic
   fighting vehicles / Michael E. Haskew.
Description: Minneapolis : Voyageur Press, [2016] | Includes index.
Identifiers: LCCN 2016001692 | ISBN 9780760350300 (plc)
Subjects: LCSH: Sherman tank–History. | Sherman tank–Pictorial works.
Classification: LCC UG446.5 .H3727 2016 | DDC 623.74/752–dc23
LC record available at http://lccn.loc.gov/2016001692

Acquiring Editor: Dennis Pernu
Project Manager: Sherry Anisi
Art Director: James Kegley
Layout: Kim Winscher

Printed in China